W9-CBN-406

From Volunteers to Leaders

The Aftermath of a Volunteer Training Program

Rev. Dr. Alex J. Moses, Sr. D.Min.

BK Royston Publishing LLC

Jeffersonville, IN

BK Royston Publishing
P. O. Box 4321
Jeffersonville, IN 47131
502-802-5385
http://bkroystonpublishing.com
bkroystonpublishing@gmail.com

© Copyright – 2015

All Rights Reserved. No part of this book may be reproduced, stored in a retrieval system, or transmitted by any means without the written permission of the author.

Published by: BK Royston Publishing LLC
Cover Design: Customwebonline.com

ISBN-13: 978-0692396742
ISBN-10: 0692396748
LCCN: 2015934796

Printed in the United States of America

Dedication

I dedicate this work to God who saved me, revealed the need of it to me, and used me in the development of it.

And, with profound love and gratitude, I dedicate this work to my loving wife, who believed I could do it, encouraged me and made the necessary sacrifices to take the pressure off me so I could complete it. Also, in loving memory of Rev. Albert E. Hampton, my closest friend, who encouraged me at the inception, and who was taken home by God, I dedicate this work.

Also, to my instructor, Dr. T. Vaughn Walker, who invited me to this new endeavor for The Southern Baptist Theological Seminary.

Finally, I dedicate this work to the Eastern Star Baptist Church, who financed this effort, and participated in the implementation of it, and to all who provided support when I was overwhelmed in an effort to complete it.

GOD BLESS YOU!

Preface

With this work having been completed, I cannot help but meditate on the experience and recall the many people who helped and supported me along the way. Others saw in me the deep yearning to gain a broader understanding of the dynamics of leadership, which would better enable me to equip God's people for service.

My wife, Trudy, listened to my concerns regarding the needs of the volunteer leadership workforce of the Eastern Star Baptist Church, and watered the thought of my pursuing a D.Min. with her words, "I know you can do it!" She has blessed and impacted my life so much that I feel that I am a better man because of her. My wife has forfeited her educational pursuits to pave the way for our children to receive their college education. I pray that I have made her happy and blessed her life as much as she has blessed my life and our children's.

Deacon Elbert Brown, a co-laborer and friend, saw the need as well, and constantly reminded me, "God will bless the church through your unselfish sacrifices."

Then, I persevered with the encouragement of Dr. T. V. Walker, my faculty supervisor, and the help of the D.Min. Faculty, including Drs. Walker, Hughes, and Lawless; faculty instructor, Mrs. Omanson; D.Min. secretary, Jeanie Knight, and, of course, Guy Fredrick who supplied the computer expertise to pull this project together.

This pursuit has been the most challenging of my life, but at no time did I consider withdrawing from the program. Because of the potential for growth that I believed such a project could provide, I labored even harder. With people like Deacon Loviest Busby, Jr., Trustee Robert Barlow, and Social Service Director Anna Beasley providing sacrificial committed service—always— as my armor bearers, when I was tied to my studies, I had no reason to turn from my educational pursuits.

God favored me with a divine call to further preparation, the church honored God's wisdom and agreed to finance it, and my loving wife helped me through it. Therefore, there are no adequate words that could express my heartfelt gratitude to all who believed in me and challenged and supported me as I endeavored to enhance my knowledge that I may be able to equip God's people for the life transforming work of the ministry.

Finally, in the words of the apostle Paul, "I thank Christ Jesus, our Lord, who hath enabled me, in that he counted me faithful, putting me into the ministry, who was before a blasphemer, and a persecutor, and injurious; but I obtained mercy, because I did it ignorantly in unbelief."

Rev. Dr. Alex J. Moses, Sr. D.Min.

Louisville, Kentucky

December 2001

BIOGRAPHY

Rev. Dr. Alex J. Moses, Sr. - (1944 -   )

Pastor – Eastern Star Baptist Church; Louisville, Kentucky for the past 30 1/2 yrs.

Native of Newberry, South Carolina, One of nine children born to the late Ira M. Moses & Carrie L. Moses. A 1964 graduate of Armstrong High School; Richmond, Virginia; and also attended Kentucky State University in Frankfort, Kentucky

His religious education includes the following:

Bachelor of Arts & Religious Education (1983) from Simmons Bible College of Louisville, Kentucky; Master of Arts Christian Education (1988) from The Southern Baptist Theological Seminary; Louisville, Kentucky; Master of Divinity Equivalent (1999); The Southern Baptist Theological Seminary Doctor of Ministry Black Church Leadership (2001) The Southern Baptist Theological Seminary
Instructor at Simmons Bible College (12 years), and Former Managerial employee at General Electric for 10 years.

Affiliations with Louisville Metro Police Department include Citizens Police Academy, Volunteer instructor - LMPD Teaching a class "Community Wins" and serves as Chair - LMPD Merit Board, and Member, Racial Fairness

Commission

Member - NAACP
Former Board Member - Louisville Urban League
Visiting Professor - University of Louisville–Topic
"Leadership" March 2008

Co-President - CLOUT - Citizens of Louisville Organized
United Together

Recognition & Awards
Honorary Doctorate - Simmons Bible College
2001 Honorary Chief of Police Award – Louisville
Division of Police
2001 Honored Volunteer Bell Award – City of Louisville
2002 Community Partnership Award – City of Louisville,
Division of Police
2003 Dr. Martin Luther King, Jr. Image Award Recipient in
Theology
2007 & 2008 & 2009 featured in the inaugural and 2nd &
3rd edition of Who's Who in Black Louisville, celebrating
African-American achievements.

September 27, 2005 featured in the NY Times Article
entitled "In Louisville: A Measured Police Response"; also
featured in the National Baptist Voice and Christianity
Today magazines.

2011 Recipient of the Robert Delahanty/Ben Shobe
Humanitarian Award

Received Tuskegee Airman Golden Image Award for
Community Leadership

2012 Louisville Defender Newspaper's Lifetime Achievement and Community Service Award for outstanding Personal and Professional commitment and unselfish contribution to the Community;

2013 HONORARY SHERIFF OF JEFFERSON COUNTY

On July 13, 2013, Howard Street was renamed in honor of Rev. Dr. Alex J. Moses, Sr. March 2014 served as the minister's coordinator for the commemorative 50 year March on Frankfort, Kentucky

Recently nominated to Kentucky Civil Rights Hall of Fame

During a time when the community was infested with drugs, gangs, violence and poverty, Dr. Moses expressed his love for people by standing up for and with the neighborhood families who faced hardships. He spearheaded the church's efforts (along with the members of the church) to buy, tear down/and or renovate homes and he even marched with various civil rights groups to oppose crime and violence in our communities.

He has been married to his wife Trudy for 50 years and they have 3 children.

One very important poetic statement that he makes is: "You are not successful unless you have successors";

Table of Contents

CHAPTER 1

INTRODUCTION

Over the years as Pastor of the Eastern Star Baptist Church, I have struggled to lead God's people to a deeper relationship in Christ, which leads to a deeper service commitment. The nature of the struggle has to do with the lack of volunteer leadership and the lack of quality leadership which volunteers are able to provide.

When questioned as to why more members in the church did not volunteer for service, many reasons were given. Some stated they had low self-esteem, did not have any leadership skills, or did not have spiritual gifts or talents. Others felt leadership was for a select few. Having been one who gave those same answers when asked to volunteer, and now after having served in various ministries, I believe there are even more influences that hinder Christians from volunteering their service and becoming committed.

Therefore, to enlighten, enlist, and enroll volunteers in leadership training and to enhance the quality of leadership being provided by existing volunteers, potential volunteers, and paid staff, this leadership training model was developed. The

Leadership Training Module is designed to strengthen God's servants in the areas of their proposed weaknesses regarding their potential to provide leadership which will equip the saints of God for the work of the ministry, and thus increase the workforce of the church and lighten the service burdens of the pastor.

The biblical foundation for the development of this training model is Exodus 18:13-26 and Ephesians 4:11-16. The Bible teaches that the church is the body of Christ having many members and not all members have the same function. With that being true, every member has significance and therefore must be sought out and equipped for service and provided opportunity to serve. Moreover, with each functioning member of the body of Christ being qualified to serve, the church will be able to accomplish greater things for the Lord.

The training sessions were made available to persons thirteen years and older, and last for five consecutive Sundays. Christians volunteer and give of their time and service more readily, after having been trained for service and provided a job description and leadership support. This is the design and ultimate goal of the Leadership Training Model; that is, equipping the saints for the work of the ministry, which will enable them to perpetuate the process.

Purpose

Over the years of Pastoring the Eastern Star Baptist Church, through participation in leadership, observation, and evaluation, this writer has concluded that the Eastern Star Baptist Church will not rise above

the quality of its leadership training. Therefore, leadership training provided for lay leaders plays a monumental role in meeting needs of the church and community. The purpose of this research and development project is to develop a training model that will enhance the quality of volunteer leadership in the Eastern Star Baptist Church, Louisville, Kentucky.

Goals

There are four desired goals of this project. The first goal is that of determining the training needs of the church's existing workforce, active volunteers, and potential volunteers participating in the survey/questionnaire. The second goal focuses on developing a training program that will address the deficiencies of the respondents that are revealed by the questionnaire answers. Goal number three seeks to enlist all who shared in the survey to participate in the actual training model that was developed as a direct response to their needs disclosed by the survey results. The fourth and final goal is the implementation of the training model. The implementation of the training model will equip participants with leadership training that will enable them to make competent decisions in leading and equipping others for service.

Background

In 1911, under the direction of the Holy Spirit, a group of Christians were led to organize a church in their community. After an extended period of meditation, prayer, and fellowship, the Eastern Star Baptist Church was born. The first meeting place was located on Kinslows Row, in an alley, an area called "The Bottoms" in the city of Louisville, Kentucky. The area was predominantly an African American community. Segregation during this period was a way of life. Employment was limited to low-paying manual labor jobs. Education was not high on the priority list; survival topped the list. Therefore, poverty, lack of training, and low self-esteem were major hindrances for the members of the church. However, God never left nor forsook the members of Eastern Star Baptist Church. The church remained standing at that location, pointing seekers to a better way of life through Jesus Christ, who is the provider of hope, help, and healing.

In 1959, the church was forced to relocate due to urban renewal. What many thought was a curse turned out to be a blessing. Not only did the church move to another edifice, the whole community followed as much as available housing allowed in the new area. Up until 1959, the church had only three pastors. The fourth pastor, led by the wisdom of God, relocated the church at 2400 Howard Street, and the church has remained there for forty years.

The current location is centrally located in the western part of the city of Louisville. The facility now occupied by the church was purchased from a white congregation. The community itself at that time was predominantly white. Over the years, the make-up of

the community has changed. It is now predominantly African American due to "white flight."

The newly acquired building provided Eastern Star with classrooms and other spaces to equip the members for service, as far as resources would allow. The church now owns other properties in the neighborhood, which includes three parking lots, a multi-purpose facility, four vacant lots, and two houses. The church employs a full time pastor and eight part-time workers. Therefore, the church is able to provide the following ministries for the community and membership: tutoring, youth groups, social services, Bible study, Sunday School, summer day camp, Vacation Bible School, senior adult ministry, clothes closet, after school activities, a girls' basketball team, computer training, community service work for young law breakers, and classes dealing with anger control and substance abuse.

Information gathered from the 1990 Census of Population and Housing by the Kentucky State Data Center of the University of Louisville states that the majority of the people in the community have a high school education, its equivalent, or less. Only small percentages have gone to college, and an even smaller number have completed a degree program.[i]

Tex Sample gives three clear lifestyle groups: cultural left, cultural middle, and cultural right.[ii] Two other divisions, which seem to identify the persons served by the church, are the Hard Living and the Desperate Poor.

The "Hard Living" folk are angry, distrustful, rebellious, anxious people who often feel left out of things. Beyond survival but still near poor, hard living people struggle to keep the little they have. With a median income of nearly half the national figure, they are often unemployed, with more than a fourth of their number seeking employment or working part-time. Their jobs are not satisfying and are typically semi-skilled or unskilled. They work with machines, manual labor, and a range of service occupations.

The "Hard Living" have large families, and a high proportion (50 percent) of the people are divorced, separated or living together unmarried. The Hard Living division represents a high percentage of minorities. Acutely aware of their low social status, they rank next to the bottom in personal happiness and deeply mistrust the system, having little confidence in politicians and corporate management.[iii]

Some subgroups in this lifestyle are (1) the "street-smart operator" who knows how to work the underground criminal economy; (2) "the crafty-Sustainer," not so much involved in criminal pursuits, but who knows how to work the system through trade offs, cash for jobs done on the side, and sometimes a stealthy maneuvering of welfare programs; (3) The "poverty-stricken sustainer" family, usually a single mother with children scratching out a meager living by parlaying a minimum wage job, food stamps, and when possible, welfare.[iv]

The "Desperate Poor" consists of approximately six million Americans who constitute the poorest of the poor. Their income never exceeds 40 percent of the national median income and nearly 80 percent receive less than a fourth of that. They are old, with an average age of sixty-six, often ill and poorly educated. Also enclosed within the "Desperate Poor" is a class known as the "Survivors," which is divided into two distinct classes, one of which are those trapped within intergenerational poverty; rarely do they escape it. The persons in this class tend to be younger than the aged poor. The second class has slipped into this condition by virtue of misfortune, a lack of effort, or the impoverishing effects of old age from which they could not protect themselves.[v]

According to the 1990 Census of Population and Housing secured by the Kentucky State Data Center of the University of Louisville, the area where the church is located the population numbers at 26,582 with the average income around $7399.[vi] These statistics are indicative of the degree of poverty that this community faces. With poverty come many problems such as illiteracy, health issues, crime, violence, substance abuse, and a lack of self-worth and internal motivation.

The Church

Although the church building is constructed

differently from any other building in the community, it is in the community for the benefit of the community. In years gone by, the church was the nucleus of the community for all functions, and now that focus is returning.

Eastern Star Baptist Church reaches out to the community as a helper, a way to the lost, a strengthening agent to the powerless, an encourager to those of low self-esteem, and a healer for the wounded. The church offers programs for all ages. The church is the community leader that will take a stand against any ills that harm the well being of the church and community.

The church does not stand idly by but is the salt and light of the earth that God is calling it to be (Matt 5:13-14).

The church has participated in drug and crime marches to let the city officials know that we are not pleased with the unlawful acts that are penetrating the community. The church participates in a local organization of churches who believe that there is strength in numbers, in order to get some things accomplished that would go unnoticed by government officials.

The church is not for the members only, but makes all ministries available to the immediate community by personal invitation, and door-to-door contact. The members go door-to-door and invite residents to attend worship and church activities. Eastern Star has a radio broadcast and makes use of other communication vehicles to promote the gospel of the Lord Jesus Christ.

The church is in the community to help those of the community. There are those who have broken the law. When the court levies punishment of community service, the church serves as the weekly meeting place for their class study program and a place to carry out their work assignment to keep offenders from doing jail time. To those who are lost, who do not know Jesus Christ and cannot find their way, the church serves as an intercessor that introduces them to Jesus Christ, the Way-Maker. Then there are those who have been hurt by the trials and tribulations of life. The church exhibits God's presence through love, encouragement, and assistance to help raise them up and start them on their way. To those who are suffering from low self-esteem because they cannot read well enough to function in society, the church offers tutoring for all ages, including adults.

The church comes out into the community in the form of a parade once a year. The Vacation Bible School Parade, as it is known, is a vehicle used to reach out to the community. As a show of "unity in the

 community," the fire department and police departments participate in the parade as time and circumstances allow. The church is in the community and takes part in community activities.

Heritage

As the new pastor of the Eastern Star Baptist Church (ESBC) in 1984, this pastor inherited many traditional practices, some good, and some bad. As an already established member of Eastern Star Baptist Church, I observed the former pastor in his efforts to stay true to the heritage passed to him as he cared for the flock. On many occasions, the church experienced turmoil relative to the problem of church tradition. The unrest was because the administration did not change the method of ministry.

The only musical instruments recognized in the church were a piano and an organ. That was an issue with younger members who wanted to use other instruments to glorify God. Biblical teachings, such as "a woman should not wear pants," were a constant issue to be dealt with. There were other traditions such as no playing of cards, or checkers. As a rule, no selling on church property was permitted. Dancing of any kind was taboo.

Church polity required new converts to be voted into the church family for baptism rather than receive them on their profession of faith. Doctrinal belief held that women were not to be preaching ministers. The deacons and trustees were considered an integral part of the tradition of the church. Midweek service, prayer meeting and Bible study, had to be on Wednesday night. The pastor, it seemed, was the primary person to visit the sick (home or hospital) and the incarcerated. The physical appearance of the pastor was one of the black suit and traditional white shirt. Colored shirts were not to be used by the pastor, especially at church functions.

The local heritage or tradition dictated church attire—putting on their "Sunday-Go-to-Meeting" clothes. The heritage of greater magnitude was wrapped up in the coming together in the community revival crusade. Also, denominational and Christian heritage dictated that the church should be aligned with local, state and national bodies that complimented the church denomination. Therefore, the ESBC is a member of the Central District Association of Baptists (local body), the General Association of Baptists in Kentucky (state body), and the National Baptist Convention USA, Inc. of the Baptist faith and practice.

Symbols and Rituals

The most recognizable symbolism in the Eastern Star Baptist Church is rooted in the sacrificial death of Christ as seen in the observance of baptism and the Lord's Supper (Communion). The act of baptism is symbolic of the believer being baptized in union with Christ. It identifies the believer's participating in the death, burial, and resurrection with Jesus Christ to the newness of life. Once baptized, the new member then receives the "right hand of fellowship."

There are pictures of a cross present in the church, which call to mind Calvary, the place where Jesus was crucified. Moreover, the unleavened bread

 and fruit of the vine are symbolic of the Lord Jesus Christ's broken body and shed blood. They are used as a reminder when commemorating what Christ did for the believer through His suffering and death. For ninety years, Eastern Star Baptist Church has maintained the ritual of serving the Lord's Supper on the second Sunday of each month preceded by a testimonial service.

The most notable ritual in ESBC is the programming order of the Sunday morning worship. The order of worship, in printed format, has had the same pattern since the origin of the church. The above traditions had been in place since the establishment of the church. However, all have been reviewed and adjustments made.

Pastor's Leadership Style

According to Ephesians 4:11, the Lord provided the church the necessary ministry gifts to equip the saints for the work of the ministry. Therefore, realizing it is the job of the pastor to do the work of equipping the leaders, he must devise a plan, enlist leaders for training, and engage in the process of leader construction and re-construction that will provide competent lay leadership.

Since this writer understands this is God's way of enlisting and training leaders; the pastoral task at Eastern Star Baptist Church is approached from a "pastor as enabler" leadership style. This leadership style is best suited for a predominantly lay leadership administration. In this style as an enabler, I seek to know first-hand whom I am leading, their past history, weaknesses and strengths, and endeavor to build the saints up to the point of a working knowledge of the church's mission in the area of administration, confidence, and courage. In providing enabling leadership, I build self-esteem, provide leadership training, and help believers discover their gifts, match gifts and talents with tasks. I am an encourager; I delegate authority. I share biblical examples of God's working through his people and seek to involve the entire church in church work and the work of the church.

Over the many years of pastoring the Eastern Star Baptist Church, I recognize now, more than ever before, that a leadership-training model must be developed and implemented to equip volunteers for the front line leadership ministry.

Throughout the history of Eastern Star, the  pastor, secretary, and janitor were the paid staff of the church, with the pastor being the only full time employee. However, in a changing society needs change, and with the changing of needs, ministries change in what they provide and the number of persons who direct them. Therefore, when the church's mission endeavors have financially outgrown the church's resources to hire additional staff, volunteers must be utilized on a much larger scale and in a more meaningful way.

At one time, the church could "get by" with the basic ministries of church life, Sunday worship, Bible study, Sunday school, and prayer meeting. But, with the emergence of so many different needs, volunteers must be utilized like never before in providing important ministry leadership.

Moreover, if volunteers are going to impact the church's mission and evangelical efforts, they must be properly trained. They must be trained to deal with problems and concerns that have to do with the people they will minister to. And training must also deal with individual feelings of inadequacy, what the volunteers have experienced and what they fear in leadership encounters. The training will afford a sense of purpose in church endeavors and a sense of purpose in the lives of volunteers who seek to meet the challenge of leadership in an effort to glorify God.

Having been frustrated over the problem of not having enough help during my pastorate at Eastern Star Baptist Church, it is now time to put a leadership-training model in place to equip volunteers to serve in positions the church cannot afford to pay hired staff. Once this leadership-training model has been developed based on the needs of potential and existing leaders; the Eastern Star Baptist Church will be in a position to enlist volunteers who can be equipped for service without fear and uncertainty. Volunteers will be encouraged to come forth. Delegation of authority will enhance growth in members who are willing to serve. The church will become membership and volunteer driven, rather than pastor driven.

The development and implementation of a leadership training model will enable the Eastern Star Baptist Church to broaden its leadership personnel, its ministries, and reach more people for Christ, church membership, Bible study, fellowship, and service. In dealing with volunteer workers, many obstacles that volunteers have shared with this pastor hinder them from serving in church leadership roles. These hindrances have to do with historical roles of volunteer leaders in the church, knowledge of God's Word and work, low self-esteem, fear of rejection, communication, conflict, management, lack of leadership training, time management, leadership assignment, etc.

The Leadership Training Model is specifically written to address these issues.

Definitions and Terms

Throughout this project words will be used that may need defining to give the reader a clearer picture. Therefore, words this author deems necessary will be listed and explained. With those words being defined, the reader will comprehend the content with clarity and develop a deeper desire within for the remaining information provided on the subject:

Volunteer/Lay Leader. Understood to mean a member of the church who renders leadership in a church having been elected by the church, volunteered, or appointed by the pastor to a specific position. The individual bearing such title receives no financial compensation, but serves in response to God's call, giftedness and blessing upon their life.

Spiritual Gifts. Special ability given by God to a believer to empower the individual to serve within the body of Christ to accomplish God's will and purpose.

Auxiliary Leadership. Understood as a lay leader who has been assigned the task of providing leadership for a support ministry of the church, which is a part or component of the overall work and purpose of the church.

Limitations

The leadership-training model for the Eastern Star Baptist Church will be made available to volunteer lay leaders beginning at age thirteen and up. Youth training will be predicated on volunteerism, personal recommendations, church election, and pastoral appointment. The instructor for the class will be the pastor or person trained in the model. Class sessions will begin each January and last six months, with two sessions taught each month. The sessions will last one and one-half hours, beginning at six p.m. and no later than seven thirty p.m. every second and fourth week of the month.

Adult leadership training sessions will be held for three months, with classes each Saturday at ten a.m. Participants of the class will be current, active and potential lay leaders. Participants must be elected to a position of service, display interest in leadership, volunteer or be appointed/recommended by the pastor. They must be members of the church, possessing qualities that demonstrate their willingness to honor God through their time, talent and treasure. The pastor will provide the instruction for the class. The class period will be two hours.

Conclusion

Chapter one has provided the contextual setting and the leadership potential needs of the volunteer workforce of the Eastern Star Baptist Church. Therefore, that information gave rise to the development of a Leadership Training Model. If this training model is to spiritually meet the needs of leadership has to be of the kind that complies with the will of God for preparing and giving direction to His people. Therefore, the revelation of God's will in His written word must be sought. It must be viewed from a Biblical, historical, and theological point of reference to gather its deeper meaning, implementation, and practice.

CHAPTER 2

BIBLICAL AND HISTORICAL LEADERSHIP TRAINING MODELS

With Chapter One having introduced and set forth directions for the leadership training model, Chapter two will deal with biblical models of leadership training for lay leaders/volunteers. Biblical models of leadership found in the Old Testament (Exodus 18:19-23) and in the New Testament (Ephesians 4:14-16) are expounded on.

These passages affirm the idea of volunteer leadership training and foundations to build upon. A theological rationale for a lay leadership development and training model will be established based on biblical principles. The first biblical passage considered is Exodus 18:19-23.

In churches where ministries are needed and limited church resources to hire professional and full-time staff are available, existing leadership must seek out God's potential in the giftedness of His people. These "God-gifted" people must be sought out, enlisted, trained, and given the opportunity to serve.

The New Testament concept of leadership training that sheds light on this project is found in Ephesians 4:11-12. It had been earlier stated that through faith in Jesus Christ, believers are created unto good works, according to Ephesians 2:10. Therefore, God's sacrificial love toward the recipients of His salvation through the redemptive work of Christ's death and resurrection calls for a response.

The Bible teaches in Ephesians 2:10
For by grace are ye saved through faith; and that not of yourselves: it is the gift of God; for we are His workmanship, created in Christ Jesus unto good works, which God hath before ordained that we should walk in them.

And in Romans 12:1,
I beseech you therefore, brethren, by the mercies of God, that ye present your bodies a living sacrifice, holy, acceptable unto God, which is your reasonable service.

Therefore, the Bible is clear on the mandate by God that all who are aligned with Him through faith must serve as leaders and practitioners of His ideology.

Effective leadership however requires leadership training for all who will volunteer. Therefore, to develop a Leadership Training Module[vii] for Eastern Star Baptist Church[viii] that will provide growth and competent leadership in volunteer leaders and potential leaders, who will in turn equip the church membership for carrying out the mission of the church, it is absolutely necessary that a training model be developed based on a sound biblical and theological premise.

The biblical perspective will provide Old and New Testament models. It will provide pertinent information on what leaders should be taught. Attention will be given to the method and principle of disseminating instruction that will enhance leadership potential. Finally, it will familiarize the reader with the task to be performed.

The Biblical Perspectives

The LTM is the process of equipping or preparing one for leadership through a specifically designed paradigm. The Old Testament Biblical foundation for developing an LTM for Eastern Star is Exodus 18:19-23. This leadership model originated out of the wise advice of Jethro.

The advice was offered to his son-in-law, Moses. Observing Moses as he judged (get justice, settle a case)[ix] the problems of the Israelites from morning to evening, Jethro saw the stress and strain encumbered upon Moses due to a monumental work load based on the length of time and the many cases brought before him as a judge. Knowing the burden of such an unhealthy task, Jethro, out of deep concern, warns Moses the responsibility is too great for him to bear alone. He, therefore, advised Moses to seek out persons he could train to be co-laborers with him in such an awesome work. Therefore, at the core of Jethro's advice was an LTM that would (1) seek volunteers, (2) train them, (3) delegate authority and responsibility relative to judging the issues of the Israelites.

If Moses took his father-in-law's counsel and implemented the recommended leadership model, his workload would be lightened and others would be trained, enabling them to help him as well as be in a position to train others and please God through serving His people. Based on the model as prescribed by Jethro, Moses would maintain his position as primary leader and final authority. More important, he would judge the most complicated and more serious cases. The process of leadership and problem solving regarding the cases of the Israelites would therefore be a remedy for Moses' administrative problem.

The inefficiency of the current judicial system as Jethro saw it is recorded in Exodus 18:17-18. The passage explains the problem in this manner.

"And Moses' father in law said unto him, the thing that thou doest is not good. Thou wilt surely wear away, both thou, and this people that is with thee: for this thing is too heavy for thee: thou art not able to perform it thyself alone."

The authority behind the recommendation, formation, and implementation of a leadership-training model as suggested by Jethro is God. Exodus 18:19 affirms that in this declaration, "And God shall be with thee: be thou for the people to Godward, that thou mayest bring the cases unto God."

The clause 'and God shall be with thee' translates, "that God may be with you."[x] Therefore, God's presence and blessing was dependent upon Moses' heeding Jethro's counsel and implementing a new way of providing a more acceptable method of

administering justice. God provided Jethro's counsel, and the cases to be dealt with were the domestic problems of the people. Thus, Moses is introduced as a Judge.[xi]

Jethro sees immediately that Moses is committed to an unworkable practice. Moses cannot handle the heavy case docket. We do not know whether Moses was so concerned with control that he wanted to handle all the cases himself, or if he was unreflective and had never thought about a more workable, practical system. Moses seems not to have had much common sense about administrative matters. But then, such dominating figures often do not. Jethro feared for Moses that he will "burn out"; Jethro's solution is that

Moses must learn to delegate.[xii]

Jethro thus proposes a judicial system, distinct from the primitive practice of one-man adjudication. The proposal included (a) recruitment of good people (v. 21); (b) their training and preparation (v. 20); (c) a system of courts for different social units (v. 21); (d) a "high court" over which Moses would preside (v. 22); and (e) continued affirmation that the entire system would be referred to the will of God (vv.19, 23).[xiii]

Perhaps the most important matter in Jethro's plan concerns the qualifications of the judges (v. 21). They are to be able, God-fearing haters of dishonest (violent) gain. This list of qualifications is both theologically referenced and aware that corruption is not likely to be about large, theological matters, but about the modest temptations of bribery and economic manipulation.[xiv] Such a system will save Moses from burnout, but more important, it will let the community go home in peace i.e., in harmony and wholeness, free of conflict, enjoying a stable, shared welfare (v. 23).[xv]

The Theological Perspective

A theological perspective on Exodus provides important information relative to the conservative understanding of the form and manner on doing something. These manners can be born out of former modes, whether psychological or social. It aids in providing a clearer and more unifying understanding of the text in its original setting.[xvi]

The Duties of the Judge. In the Old Testament, the judge's responsibility was two-fold: (1) inquire of God; (2) settle disputes. The Hebrew word 'dabak' may mean to tread in the sense of resorting to a place (Deuteronomy 12:5).[xvii] In the vast majority of the cases it came to mean seeking, consulting, or inquiring of the Lord, although it also had other related meanings (to inquire, investigate, and demand). Dispute translates as 'dabar', which most often means word. Dabar came to be used in a very general way of any matter or affair about which one speaks.

The Judge

Cases brought before the judges can be categorized as business, affair, events, and cause. First Samuel 21:8 provides an example of a "business dispute". That passage states, "And David said unto Ahimelech, and is there not here under thine hand spear or sword? For I have neither brought my sword not my weapons with me, because the king's business require haste." "Acts" can be related to the functions of an individual. This idea can be gleaned from 1 Kings 11:41 where it is stated, "And the rest of the acts of Solomon, and all that he did, and his wisdom, are they not written in the book of the acts of Solomon?"

A case regarding an "affair" is recorded in 1 Kings 15:5 in these words, "Because David did that which was right in the eyes of the Lord, and turned not aside from anything that he commanded him all the days of his life, save only in the matter of Uriah the Hittite." Genesis 15:1 speaks to the issue of "events." The verse declares, "After these things the word of the Lord came unto Abram in a vision, saying, 'Fear not, Abram: I am thy shield, and thy exceeding great reward.'" Then there was a cause or case for judicial investigation.

Exodus 18:16 provides insight relative to the role of the judge in dealings with those kinds of matters. Therein is stated, "When they have a matter, they come unto me; and I judge between one and another, and I do make them know the statutes of God, and his laws."

Therefore, based on the aforementioned situations, the

judge dealt with anything that arose between people.

This is confirmed by Exodus 22:8-9 which states:

If the thief be not found, then the master of the house
shall be brought unto the judges, to see whether he have
put his hand unto his neighbour's goods. For all manner
of trespass, whether it be for ox, for ass, for sheep, for
raiment, or for any manner of lost things, which another
challengeth to be his, the cause of both parties shall
come before the judges; and whom the judges shall
condemn, he shall pay double unto his neighbor.[xviii]

And also in Exodus 24:14
And he said unto the elders, Tarry ye here for us, until
we come again unto you: and, behold, Aaron and Hur
are with you: if any man have any matters to do, let him
come unto them.[xix]

Hence, the word 'matters', is in this instance

rather colorless. It suggests no connotation of strife or

dispute as such, but referred to anything that arose

between people. One would assume, however, that such

decisions were argumentative in nature.[xx]

Historical Perspectives

When God created all things, He brought into

being an orderly universe. With the creation of man

and the multiplication of people throughout the earth,

God ordained government for societies and nations.[xxi]

At first, the governmental administration of Israel was

very simple. Moses was the God-appointed leader to whom was delegated all authority over God's people. But he soon discovered that there were too many people to rule, and he was busy all day long. Jethro, his father-in-law, suggested that Moses appoint judges to rule over groups of thousands, and tens. With God's approval, Moses chose from among the heads of families.[xxii]

As already established; a judicial system was in place. However, to determine whether Moses, in his administrative endeavors utilized it properly can be determined only by studying the historical perspective of the practice of it. By doing so, we will discover (1) Jethro's knowledge of the system; (2) Moses' understanding of it; (3) his application of it, and the results of his use of it as he practiced it.[xxiii]

Though the laws of the Bible are firm, they point to God who cares about human beings personally, and therefore directs how they should live so as to please Him and enjoy His favor. Bible scholars call this the apodictic form of law, because it demonstrates how God governs His people. Apodictic comes from the Greek word apodeiktikos, which means 'demonstrative'.[xxiv]

The Bible says to obey its laws because they are God's commands. Such a statement is called a motive clause, because it blesses those who obey God's law and curses those who disobey it, or both (e.g., Lev 26)[xxv]

God told Moses how the people of Israel should live,

 and Moses recorded these commands in the first five books (The Pentateuch) of the Old Testament. These laws teach us a great deal about the Old Testament society; but they also suggest how our own society should work. God still expects His people to honor Him in their dealings with one another. The laws of the Old Testament teach us to lift up God and respect the rights of our neighbors. As interpreted by Jesus and His apostles, they form the foundation of modern Christian living.[xxvi]

Moses is quite clear that the concern for justice is not simply political pragmatism, but derives from and belongs to the very character of God. Jethro asks Moses why he shoulders such an impossible burden. In his answer, Moses asserts that he is preoccupied with "inquiries of God" (i.e., pronouncing oracles from God) and instruction (torah) of God (vv. 15-16).

And Moses said unto his father in law, because the people come unto me to inquire of God: When they have a matter, they come unto me; and I judge between one and another, and I do make them know the statutes of God, and his laws.[xxvii]

Moses is not dispensing mere practical advice or positive law but the very torah of God. The God of Israel cares about the concrete, day-to-day matters of justice.[xxviii]

The principles of delegation and empowerment are not new. After the Exodus, Moses was responsible for leading the children of Israel to the Promised Land. One responsibility was to make decisions regarding disputes between the people. The only problem was that there were millions of people! Moses sat from morning to evening settling argument (Exodus 18:13-16).[xxix]

Leaders wear out their followers and themselves when they try to lead alone. Too many church leaders suffer burnout because they think they are the only ones who can do the job. Owning responsibility for a task does not mean you alone can do the task. Servant leaders know they are most effective when they trust others to work with them. Good leaders train and empower capable people to help them carry out their responsibilities.[xxx]

Moses listened to his father-in-law. He taught the people and appointed judges over the nation. Moses delegated responsibility and authority to judges to meet the needs of the people. Carl George calls this "The Jethro Principle." George believes this method of delegating ministry still works in the church today. According to him, it is the best way to care for large numbers of people.[xxxi]

Ephesians

Chapter 4:11-16 is classified as "the church's vocation as Christ's body."[xxxii] Therefore, this division of the letter provides insight as to how the church is to function practically as Paul sets before the believers the prerequisites of Christian behavior and deportment in performing their task in the world.

The Biblical Perspective

The fundamental thought of the passage is highlighted in the very first verse. In verse one, Paul exhorts the believers to be loyal to their calling. The word, therefore, connects Paul's appeal with what has gone on before (as in Rom 12:1; Col 3:1; 1

Thessalonians 4:1). The Christian's 'calling' is God's summons to the unbeliever answered as conversion (Phil 3:14) and his/her response is to be worked out in his/her subsequent behavior patterns.

Ephesians 4:11-16 provides the church, the body of Christ, which the book of Ephesians portrays, with a New Testament leadership model. This model is within the context of this passage of scripture:

"And He gave some, apostles; and some, prophets; and some, evangelists; and some, pastors and teachers; for the perfecting of the saints, for the work of the ministry, for the edifying of the body of Christ; till we all come in the unity of the faith, and the knowledge of the Son of God, unto a perfect man, unto the measure of the stature of the fulness of Christ; that we henceforth be no more children tossed to and fro, and carried about with every wind and doctrine, by the sleight of men, and cunning craftiness, whereby they lie in wait to deceive. But speaking the truth in love, may grow up into Him in all things, which is the head, even Christ: From whom the whole body fitly joined together and compacted by that which every joint supplieth, according to the effectual working in the measure of every part, maketh increase of the body unto the edifying of itself in love."

Not only does the text give evidence of a leadership-training model but also provides the structure, organization, and administrative aspects of it. God provides the positions and the gifts as well as the curriculum and purpose needed to equip others. Therefore, this passage (4:11-16) is presented as an exhortation by God to utilize the gifts God has blessed mankind with to equip volunteers to do the work of the ministry.

The Gifts

In l Corinthians 14:4ff, the gifts of the Spirit are endowments bestowed by Him upon individual Christians, which they are expected to be exercised in the Church. The gifts of the ascended Christ are the individual Christians who are thus endowed, bestowed by Him upon the church. An honorable status indeed is conferred on those who exercise their special ministries in the church when they are presented to the church as gifts imparted to her by her exalted Lord.[xxxiii]

The second pair of gifts, evangelists and pastor-teachers (or teaching pastors), is required in each generation. The church can never dispense with men who preach the gospel and bring men and women to knowledge of truth, nor yet with men who can teach

40

and guide in the way of truth those who have been evangelized and converted.[xxxiv]

The gifts mentioned are not the only ones bestowed by Christ upon the church but these are of the first importance. Moreover, their purpose is to equip the saints for the work of service, for building up the body of Christ. The healthy growth of the believing community is the aim in view in all ministries, which the Lord has entrusted to His people.[xxxv]

Here, gifted believers are bestowed on the church. The five gifts listed can be summarized in this way: (1) The gifts are by God's design and are to be used by the apostles to guide the infant church in the way it ought to go. (2) The prophets are endowed by God to guard the infant church in what it ought to know. (3) God gives the gift of evangelizing for the purpose of dealing with sinners. (4) Pastors are called and gifted to tend the flock of God, and (5) teachers are gifted and called to teach the flock of God.

Though verses 11-16 of chapter four is the primary focus of the New Testament training model, it is necessary to highlight the word gift in verse 7. The word gift illuminates the focal passage. It works in conjunction with the word grace. ÷Üñéò in Greek

41

(grace) denotes referring to the spirit's gifts to the church. Other references to the gifts as received from the spirit are recorded in Romans 12:3ff, and 1 Corinthians 12:4ff.[xxxvi] Therefore, Paul is addressing the contribution believers are to make as members of the body of Christ. In essence, every Christian is given a gift by the grace of God to build others up, therefore edifying God.[xxxvii]

Now in verse 11, the grace of gifts mentioned are regarding the church's work. The list includes apostles, prophets, evangelists, pastors, and teachers. The most prominent of the list however were the apostles and prophets according to Ephesians 2:20 where it is states, "and are built upon the foundation of the apostles and prophets, Jesus himself being the chief corner stone."[xxxviii]

In the early church, the apostles and prophets bore witness to the incarnated and risen Lord and were the instruments God used to further express His thoughts to His church. The evangelist was not considered an office, but a ministry or function.[xxxix]

In defining the role(s) of the pastors and teachers, it appears synonymous with each other, meaning persons holding such position performed the same functions.[xl]

In verses 12 and 13, Paul endeavors to define

the purpose of gifts in the church. All believers may be equipped (qualified) by the function which his servants perform in order that they in turn may discharge their service as Christians in the world. The consequence is that by this interplay of a regular ministry, ordained and appointed by the head of the church, and the rank and file of the church, Christ's body may be built up.[xli]

Verse 13 expresses the anticipated end results of God utilizing the gifts in the people who have been endowed with them to bring all into the unity of the faith. That is that all believers may have a deeper understanding of Christ, His church and His work. By having a more thorough understanding, growth will occur.[xlii]

Verses 14 and 15 shed light on the benefits of such growth. In other words, believers will respond in a mature manner to various tests of their faith and not display infant symptoms. False doctrine and false teachers will not lead them astray.[xliii]

In the concluding verse of this New Testament Leadership Training Model, it is clear that the church, Christ's body, has many members, though different from each other, have very important parts to play in connection with each other and the overall function of the church. Moreover, due to the divine intervention of Christ, through the gifts in the members of the body working jointly with each other, each part works properly. Therefore, by the unifying operation, the whole body is edified (built up), as love becomes the 'atmosphere' in which this process of mutual encouragement and responsibility is exercised, with each part of the church playing the role appointed for it.[xliv]

The Theological Perspective

Jesus has commissioned the church to "make disciples of all the nations" (Matt 28:19). Some limit this statement to a ministry of evangelism. Others emphasize the educational ministry of the local church.[xlv]

Another aspect of our commission includes helping individuals to discover, develop, and use their spiritual gifts, for it is through these that believers will be able to disciple others for Jesus. But most Christians are unaware of the biblical teachings about spiritual gifts and their relationship to the local church. Here are some of those principles.[xlvi]

Spiritual Gifts

Scripture makes it very clear; God wants you to know about your spiritual gifts. First Corinthians 12:1 states: "Now concern spiritual gifts, brethren, I do not want you to be unaware." The tragedy of the average church is that its members do not know they are gifted. According to the Bible, every believer is gifted by the Holy Spirit (1 Pet 4:10). Yet, statistically speaking, "Do you think that 20 percent of these believers are using their gifts?"[xlvii] When a church

45

ignores the importance of spiritual gifts, dissension may

 creep into the church. When members do not understand the biblical teaching of gifts, they may begin to compete with one another. xlviii

When a church ignores the importance of spiritual gifts, programs may become all important. The church's vision is not on a man's spiritual gifts, it is usually on program. Instead of asking, "What needs do we have? What gifts do we have to meet our needs?" It asks, "What kind of exciting program can we offer to keep people coming?" The result is an entertainment binge competing with other churches as well as with the professionalism of the world.xlix Gifts have two basic purposes in the church. Gifts are to produce growth. Gifts are not for one's private use. They are to be shared, not hoarded. l

Another purpose of the gifts is to produce unity. The Holy Spirit has not given gifts to produce competition. His purpose was to produce contribution and thus a unity of spirit.li Each member of the body of

Christ is necessary. "For the body is not one member, but many. If the foot should say, 'Because I am not the hand, I am not a part of the body,' it is not for this reason any less a part of the body. If the whole body were an eye, where would the hearing be? If the whole were hearing, where would the sense of smell be? . . . and the eye cannot say to the hand, 'I have no need of you,' or again the head to the feet, 'I have no need of you'" (1 Corinthians 12:14-17. 29).[lii] Gifts differ. Some members of the body are more obvious. Some members are more vital to life than others, but each member is responsible to fulfill his or her own function.[liii]

Public understanding of spiritual gifts should eliminate inferiority feelings. No matter how often you say that every member of the body of Christ is essential, there are those who cannot accept the fact. Some claim they are too old to be useful. Others claim they are not educated enough. Others say they are too young.[liv] This is self-deception. It is false humility. It is not only unbiblical, it is anti-biblical. There is no need for anyone in the body of Christ to feel inferior.[lv]

Proper understanding of spiritual gifts should eliminate exaggerated self-esteem. There are those in the church who consider themselves above the average

church member. They are self-satisfied. They feel they
have reached a level of maturity, ability, or knowledge

far ahead of the rest. They sit back, relax, and coast
along. They watch from the outside and pass down
judgments of approval or disapproval on what is
happening.[lvi] Spiritual gifts should be used to help us
care for one another. "That there should be no division
in the body, but that the members should have the same
care for one another" (1 Corinthians 12: 25). We care
by sharing others' burdens. "Bear one another's
burdens, and thus fulfill the law of Christ" (Gal 6:2).
This means that we have to become honest enough and
humble enough to admit burdens and problems.[lvii]

The church should seek for the better gifts.[lviii]
Gifts are effective to the degree that they are used in
love. Some people use their gifts exclusively for
personal entertainment (i.e., gift of music) or personal
satisfaction (i.e., gift of helps, working around the
house). Some use their gifts primarily for status or

acceptance (i.e., gift of preaching, teaching, counseling, administration, leadership). Some just like to be seen and admired by others (i.e., gift of music, giving, showing mercy, faith).[lix]

In 1 Corinthians 13:1-3, Paul outlines the gifts in four categories and concludes that the use of any of these gifts without love is meaningless.[lx] A public gift (v.1): "If I speak with the tongues of men and angel, but do not have love, I have become a noisy gong or a clanging cymbal.[lxi] A helpful gift (v. 2a): "And if I have the gift of prophecy, and know all mysteries and all knowledge . . . but do not have love, I am nothing."[lxii] A powerful gift (v. 2b): "And if I have all faith, so as to remove mountains, but do not have love, I am nothing."[lxiii] A sacrificial gift (v. 3): "And if I give all my possessions to feed the poor, and if I deliver my body to be burned, but do not have love, it profits me nothing.[lxiv]

Gifts of the Holy Spirit are not an end in themselves. They are vehicles through which we express love to one another.[lxv]

Congregations should seek gifts according to god's priority system. First on God's priority list is that the church pursues love. God judges a church's discipleship on the basis of the member's love for each other, not on the number or quality of their gifts.[lxvi]

Historical Perspective

Ephesians 4:1-16 concentrates heavily on the church. In fact, no other section of the letter is so directly and intensively devoted to the church's life and purpose. The church is the sphere into which the readers have entered through their faith and baptism, the context in which they live out their calling. The major image for this community, as earlier in the letter, is that of the body verses 4, 12, 16, and as earlier, this image can be combined with the language of building (12, 16). The church is also the fullness of Christ (v 13), again taking up an earlier description, and in its final state can be seen as the mature person. All this is part of a dynamic picture of a corporate entity, which grows as its individual members are involved in a continual process of mutual adjustment and which is on the move toward unity, completeness, maturity and conformity to Christ.[lxvii]

The combination of chapter 4:11-16 is that of highlighting the significant roles of certain people who have been gifted by God to teach others in such areas of ministry that they will be able to perform the work of the ministry.[lxviii] The position of the evangelists, pastors and teachers of the writer's own time are also strengthened by their being listed alongside the foundational apostles and prophets. In this writer's perspective, the gifts of the exalted Christ come in the form of particular people and these ministers are Christ's means of equipping the church to attain its goals of unity and maturity. They are to bring both individual believers and the entire church to a state of completion.[lxix]

The purpose involved (4:12) "for the perfecting of the saints, for the work of the ministry for the edifying of the body of Christ." The word translated "perfecting" (êáôáñôéóìüò) only occurs here. The thought behind the word êáôáñôéóìüò is that of making something fully ready, perfectly equipping someone, of fully preparing something. The proper use of the gifts is to bring the body of Christ to its full potential.[lxx]

The universal gifts that God has given to the church are intended to build up the local church and the universal church. The Holy Spirit does not intend that those with these gifts should monopolize the ministry. Gifted people should help equip others to carry out the work of winning people to Christ, shepherding the flock and teaching God's word.[lxxi]

Paul used the verb 'build up' in arguing that love should govern relationships among members of the church.[lxxii] Spiritual gifts are for the common good of the church. God gives members of the church gifts to equip and build up the body of Christ. Spiritual gifts are not for pride but for service.[lxxiii]

The Leadership Style of Jesus

In an effort to develop an LTM and with it being built upon biblical and theological principles, it is necessary to give major consideration to the leadership style of Jesus. The situation of leadership at Eastern Star has similar conditions to that of Jesus' leadership endeavors. He had no paid staff, nor highly trained members. Nevertheless, the mandate upon the church to advance the cause of Christ and glorify the name of God was the epitome of the work to be done.

This being so, Jesus became the greatest and most inspiring leader in history.

With every Christian being called upon and gifted by God to do a certain service/ministry for Him, teaching and training will ensure a greater success in the performance of that duty. In addition, all who will volunteer to serve must be provided appropriate leadership training in their field of service.[lxxiv]

The leadership style of Jesus was that of a servant leader. Though it seems oxymoronic, servant leadership was the core of Jesus' style. He provided help and guidance for those who sought his help. Jesus knew his servant leadership was different. To illustrate that, he compared his example to more traditional leadership.

"You know that in this world kings are tyrants and officials lord it over the people beneath them. But among you it should be quite different. Whoever wants to be leader among you, must be your servant" (Matt 20:25-26 NLT).[lxxv]

Servant leadership as demonstrated by Jesus is not only about washing feet, it is also about leading followers into commitment, dedication, discipline, and excellence.[lxxvi]

C. Gene Wilkes, in *Jesus on Leadership*, states, "The essential lesson I learned from Jesus on leadership was that he taught and embodied leadership as service." Jesus was a servant leader in every sense of the concept. I would describe him as one who served his mission (in biblical language, "the will of [His] Father") and led by serving those he recruited to carry out that mission.[lxxvii]

Seven Principles to Lead as Jesus Led

Jesus' leadership style was one that was depicted as a servant. To prepare himself for service, Jesus humbled himself and allowed God to exalt him; Jesus was not self-seeking, but followed his Father's will rather than seeking a position; Jesus defined greatness as being a servant and being first as becoming a slave; Jesus risked serving others because He trusted that he was God's son; Jesus left his place at the head table to serve the needs of others; Jesus shared the responsibility and authority with those He was called to lead; and Jesus built a team to carry out a worldwide vision. [lxxviii]

Jesus' leadership style not only had elements of servant hood, but humility, self-sacrifice, commitment and he sought to equip others so as to enable them to advance the cause and kingdom of God

54

His Father. Jesus did just that. He was a mentor/guide. Mentors lead others through new terrain because they have been there before. Servant leaders show their followers what to do by doing it first; a mentor's actions weigh as heavily as words.[lxxix]

Jesus mentored his disciples by teaching them. Matthew 5, 6 and 7 records Jesus' "design for discipleship". He taught how kingdom people live. Jesus taught his disciples about humility, greatness and being first in line. Jesus also mentored his followers by demonstrating the power of God in their lives. That type of leadership and teaching was made available to the followers of Christ because Jesus was more spiritual, mature, and experienced, therefore, he could show others the way.[lxxx]

Conclusion

It is evident based of such scriptures as Ephesians 2:10 and Romans 12:1 that God designed His mission of redemption and reconciliation to include those who embrace Him through faith and made themselves available to serve. This is also discernable in the plight of Jesus in regards to dealing with His followers. They were always present with Him during almost every encounter in His earthly life as spectator or participant.

Therefore, to further His mission in His absence, He equipped them in that way. The success of God's mission through the followers of Christ was due in large to the reaching and teaching of Christ of those who were willing to be trained and serve.

Therefore, the ultimate goal of servant leadership is that of multiplying the workforce, equipping them to serve and delegating responsibility. Without those designs, one cannot be a successful leader because there will be no successors.

With that in mind, the desired goal in developing a leadership-training model is that of equipping the existing workforce to enlist and train others for the work of the ministry. By doing so, the workforce will be multiplied. This will provide the church with future qualified leadership that will lighten the workload of the pastor and the faithful few who always make themselves available to serve.

Moreover, the LTM will tear down barriers that have hindered many who have voiced negative reasons for not volunteering. Those who lack knowledge will receive it. Those who need encouragement will be encouraged. Those who feel torn down through prior encounters will be built up. Many will discover their gifts.

This pastor feels that every gift God has blessed the church with should be utilized in the advancement of the church. With an LTM in place to aid in cultivating those gifts, Eastern Star will experience a greater degree of spirituality, fellowship, worship, and service to God and the community.

CHAPTER 3

EXISTING VIEW AND DISCIPLINES OF LEADERSHIP

Matthew 28:18-20 records the mission of the church in this manner:

"And Jesus came and spake unto them saying, all power  is given unto me in heaven and in earth. Go ye therefore, and teach all nations, baptizing them in the name of the Father, and of the Son, and of the Holy Ghost: teaching them whatsoever I have commanded you: and, lo, I am with you always, even unto the end of the world. Amen."

However, "effective, dynamic leadership" is the greatest need of the church today. Without it our churches will never reach their full potential and we'll never reach the world for Christ.[lxxxi] Too often, our churches are bringing up the rear instead of pushing back the frontier. They are dragging behind instead of forging ahead, because leaders aren't leading.[lxxxii] Therefore, the question is, "What is the problem with church leadership? Do leaders know their roles? And, if so, why aren't they leading effectively?" These questions must be addressed.

59

Defining Leadership

The following are some representative

definitions of leadership in secular literature.

"Leadership is the process of influencing the activities of
another individual or group in efforts toward
accomplishing goals in a given situation; a learned
behavioral skill which includes the ability to help others
to achieve their potential as individuals and team
members; . . . the activity of influencing people to strive
willingly for group objectives; and an interpersonal
influence exercised in a situation and directed, through
the communication process, toward the attainment of a
special goal, or goals."[lxxxiii]

From these and other academic definitions of

leadership, three elements keep emerging: ability,

activity, and influencing. A synonym for these three

words could be persuasion. From these elements, one

could say that leadership comprises qualities and skills

in the leader's actions and behaviors that cause people

to respond. Leadership is the ability and the activity of

influencing people and shaping their behavior.

Myles Monroe defines the word leadership as

one who guides by influence, or one who directs, by

going before or along with. Regardless of title, you

cannot be a leader without followers. In essence, a

person who has subordinates but no followers is not a

leader. Subordinates who are not followers may be

viewed as a resource to be managed, rather than followers to be led. Simply put, a leader is one who leads others to leadership.[lxxxiv]

A leader is one who influences others to follow after him to a common cause or purpose, and possesses the character which inspires their confidence. At the same time, he is a confident servant. Ultimately, a leader is one who becomes himself fully and attempts to express that self totally.[lxxxv]

Ten Observations about Leadership

Leadership is described by ten views. They provide a clear understanding of what leadership is and is not. They are:

Leadership needs to be demythologized.
We need to take much of the mystery out of the subject of leadership. For example, some feel that leaders are born, while it is clear today that most of the skills of leadership can be learned. Some associate leadership with a particular type of personality; yet leaders have all different types of personalities, just as they are male and female, young and old, from all national, racial, ethnic, and cultural backgrounds.

People too often think of a leader as the solo leader, when most effective leadership involves a team. People associate leadership and power in a way that is often oversimplified. As a study of college presidents pointed out, leaders such as presidents have far more power than they think, but much less power than others tend to think they have. The power of leaders is never a generic power, but always a power related to interrelationships with others.

Leadership is not simple. Lovett Weems, in *Church Leadership: Vision, Team, Culture, and Integrity*, attempts to make leadership as neat, orderly, and understandable as possible. One needs always to remember that leadership is hardly neat, orderly, and understandable. Leadership is extremely complex and ambiguous. Leadership is filled more with frustration and joy than with order and clarity.

Michael D. Cohen and James G. March have concluded that both observers and practitioners "underestimate the complexity of leadership processes and situations and overestimate the significance of individual leaders." "Part of my excitement in living," says Greenleaf, "comes from the belief that leadership is so dependent on spirit that the essence of it will never be capsuled or codified. Leadership is truly one of the giftings of God.

Leadership is spiritual. Leadership and the spirit are closely related. Leadership is a spiritual experience and endeavor. Leadership is not a science, even if it appears to be at times. The more one works at leadership, studies leadership, and gains experience in leadership, the better leader one will be. Nevertheless, the effective leader relies not so much on effort,

education, or experience, but on judgment, feeling, sense, values, and intuition. In essence, we are talking about a kind of discernment one can only understand in spiritual terms applied to the principles of leadership within the local church and by the local pastor.

Leadership is about group purpose. Leadership is always for people and group purpose. Leadership never occurs in a vacuum, but always within an organization, a group, a community, a context. A church leader of another era liked to say that a locomotive can go faster by itself, but the task of the locomotive is to pull a train. This is the task of a leader. Helen Doohan in her study, *Leadership in Paul*, points out that Paul's leadership was enhanced not only by his ability to assess a situation correctly, but also by his ability to listen and to be perceived as a servant of the community.

Leadership is chaotic. Someone has observed that for leaders, much of the time most things are out of control. One of Terry Deal's marvelous definitions of leadership is that the task of the leaders is "the ability to be out of control comfortably." For leaders life is never simple, and important issues are never all settled at once. The effective leader is closer to the mission of the organization and its current reality, and so will identify new and potentially problematic issues to keep the group moving toward the mission.

Leadership is funny. It is almost impossible to consider the possibility of an effective leader who does not have a working sense of humor. Leadership is funny. To be so serious that one misses the humor in it, especially that which comes as a result of and at the expense of the leader, is a great loss.

Without a sense of humor, the leader not only misses an important element of leadership, but also misses the release that humor brings.

Most research about leadership is not taking place in the church. Most of the best research and writing on leadership in recent years has not been done in the context of the church or not-for-profit institutions. Those in business have done most of this work, followed by those in politics and government. Research into leadership practice has been performed mostly in the secular company setting.

Any learning about leadership is only a beginning. What you gain should be seen as a beginning of a lifelong education in leadership. One should have as a goal to make some new discovery about one's own work in leadership everyday.

Leadership is an art. The more one learns about leadership, the more one realizes that it is far more an art than a science. Leadership, like art, can be demonstrated. Leadership is like beauty: it is hard to define, but you know it when you see it.

Leadership is never an end in itself. Leadership can never be understood apart from mission and vision. Leadership never exists for itself or for the glorification or even personal development of the leader. Leadership exists to make possible a preferred future (vision) for the people involved, which reflects the heart of the mission and values to which they are committed. One can manage and administer without a real sense of spiritual direction, but one cannot lead in this manner. One can only lead in relationship to those things for which one can sincerely say, "I have a dream that someday. . . ."[lxxxvi]

The Crisis in Leadership

No matter how you choose to measure success, leadership is a key ingredient to being successful. In mountaineering, the lives of all the climbers may depend on it. Churches without it drift aimlessly, and nations have fallen for lack of it. Effective leadership is a key to success in all of life.[lxxxvii]

Our world faces a leadership crisis–in government, business, education, church, and every other sector of society, both public and private. Many people see the crisis as a problem, but it also can be interpreted as an opportunity. Seen as an opportunity, a crisis is a gift to help us find new and better ways to develop dynamic, effective leaders.[lxxxviii]

As Pastor of Eastern Star, and having provided leadership in the corporate world, there is an undying influence in me to raise the standard of church

leadership. However, resources are not available to hire properly trained staff. Nevertheless, there are members available and willing to be trained. These persons are gifted and must be trained for leadership. Therefore, an LTM is an absolute necessity. While some are willing, they lack much in training. Others are unwilling and feel training would help encourage them to volunteer.

Personal Experience in Leadership

Based on personal experience as a lay leader in the church, and currently as pastor of Eastern Star Baptist Church, my observational definition of existing leadership in the church is (1) willing but unable, (2) ill equipped to lead independently, (3) dependable but needs constant supervision, (4) possess much zeal but have little leadership knowledge, and (5) lack the vision of the greater purpose for which leadership is provided. Moreover, there is present in current leadership, self-exhortation; disregard for protocol; vulnerability to being easily persuaded; and there is no sense of urgency; and a lack of knowledge of their personal skills.

However, in regard to the above positive and negative characteristics, an LTM could work to alleviate many of the problems associated with volunteerism. Volunteers play an integrate part in kingdom building because they are God's gifts to the church. Therefore, whenever volunteers are not adequately trained and utilized in furthering God's cause, the primary leader and the church as a whole suffer. In addition, with an LTM developed and implemented, volunteers could be equipped to provide the church with quality and relative leadership that will encourage the enlistment and participation of other volunteers.

The Goals of a Leadership Training Model

The goal of the LTM is to produce exemplary leadership. Therefore, the model must have as its example Jesus and His principles. C. Gene Wilkes states regarding his work on *Jesus on Leadership*, "Too many works start with characteristics of a leader and then, if at all, move to Jesus' life and teaching to support those ideas."[lxxxix]

As long as church members revere a worldly model of leadership more than Jesus' example and teaching, then misunderstanding and conflict will occur. On the other hand, when a church chooses to follow a biblical model of servant leadership for all its leaders, God will work in amazing ways through those leaders.[xc] The challenge is to make Jesus' example the guide and focus of leadership among God's people.

The church, though in the world, is not to be operated on worldly models and principles of leadership. Many churches struggle because of the lack of servant leaders. In too many churches today, head tables have replaced the towel and washbasin as symbols of leadership among God's people. Often those recognized as leaders in the church hold positions elected by friends and family. Some of these leaders love sitting at head tables and never go near the kitchen (or nursery). Churches, however, need leaders who know how God has made and gifted them for service and who serve Christ's body. Churches need leaders who have the skills to equip others to team with them in ministry.[xci]

Because leadership is an attitude as well as an action, it must be distinguished from management. While there are certain functional similarities in both leadership and management, leadership has distinctive characteristics. It is unfortunate these distinctives so often receive little attention in developing an organizational philosophy and training an organization's executive personnel. Christian organizations are no exception.[xcii]

Leadership Distinctive

What then are some of the distinctive of leadership? Leadership can be distinguished from management by the following distinctions. They are leadership is a quality; management is a science and an art. Leadership provides vision; management supplies  realistic perspectives. Leadership deals with concepts; management relates to functions. Leadership exercises faith; management has to do with fact. Leadership seeks for effectiveness; management strives for efficiency. Leadership is an influence for good among potential resources; management is the coordination of available resources organized for maximum accomplishment. Leadership provides direction; management is concerned about control; and leadership thrives on finding opportunity; management succeeds on accomplishment. [xciii]

In the church's search for leaders, a biblical foundation and process must be followed in order to achieve results that will edify the body of Christ. The Bible is filled with examples of God's searching for leaders, and when they were found, they were used to full limit as they met His spiritual requirements, despite their human failings.[xciv]

If the church is to please God in carrying out His purpose and mission in the world, every gift must be used to its fullest potential as possible. As trends change, leadership must take on new styles and approaches. If leaders allow themselves to become isolated in the problems and perspectives of leadership, they lose touch with those whom they claim to lead. This is a subtle thing that can easily happen. When they lose contact with people and society, they no longer understand and they become ineffective.

The leader who leads must understand the culture, which comes from reading, listening, visiting, and observing. The leader learns to understand people by going where they work, visiting in their homes, sharing their joys and sorrows, and sticking close enough that leadership is not divorced from followship. There is no other way. The Bible is the church's guide. This direction, which people need, must come from the top. God has ordained this and scripture teaches it in many ways. In Christian organizations there appears to be a recurring tendency to forget this.[xcv]

In view of the information gathered it gives some insight and the definition of leadership can be influenced by one's relationship with the world or with God. If one is persuaded by the world's view, then it is a leader who lords it over those whom he or she leads. But, if Christ is the Lord of one's life, then that person must be made aware of the principles of servant leadership. This form of leadership is the type that should be taught in the church in an effort to inform, empower, and increase the workforce of the church. This is the goal of this project, developing an LTM for the Eastern Star Baptist Church, Louisville, Kentucky.

If the definition of leadership, example of Christ, and His principles are utilized to develop an LTM for Eastern Star, many traditional practices will be abandoned. Such as the pastor having to oversee everything, doing all the preaching, teaching, and visitation will ceased to be common practice. Others will be revised and many volunteers and would be volunteers will be equipped to serve with confidence. Thus quality leadership, an intimate experience with Christ, a committed life, and the product of a quality

LTM built on the sacrificial example of the Lord Jesus Christ will result.

However, current leadership trends in Eastern Star are still in a primitive state in some spheres of church organization and administration. Eastern Star still operates to some degree on the idea "use what you have" and "if it's not broken, don't fix it." However, the Bible teaches, "Where there is no vision, the people perish (Proverbs 29:28)." If there is no vision for the future, using what is available is quite adequate, because satisfaction has set in.

In addition, when the church has come into the knowledge that it has been challenged to meet diverse needs, the church must identify available resources and people to do ministry. Therefore, the church must change from just using what it has to equipping what it has to provide compatible service.

Hindrance

The following are the most predominant hindrances to volunteer leadership in the Eastern Star Baptist Church:

Volunteer leader's self-perception. If a leader's self-perception is poor, that leader will not perform based on their own will but will be influenced by outside forces. They will be controlled by the perception that others have of them. A good self-perception is absolutely necessary for good followship.

Volunteer leader's attitude toward leadership. Potential volunteers are hesitant in making a decision to volunteer themselves for service as leaders; most disquieted by the thought of the cost one has to pay to be a leader. They are apprehensive because they feel it is a high price to pay due to the rejection, resentment, alienation, and constant scrutiny by those being led.

Lack of volunteer leadership training. A lack of leadership training has always been on the hindrance list of all who give reasons for not volunteering. It is not likely that people will volunteer when there is no training program available for the preparation for the job assignment or no mention of training at all.

Volunteer's attitude toward followers. When there is a poor, bad or misinterpreted understanding follower, the leader can lead with the wrong attitude; and when the attitude is wrong, it will manifest itself in negative leadership.

Traditional leadership styles. In his book *Dying for Change*, Leith Anderson, states "as trends change, leadership must take on new styles and approaches." If leaders allow themselves to become isolated in the problems and perspectives of leadership, they lose touch with those whom they claim to lead. This is a subtle thing that can easily happen. When they lose contact with people and society, they no longer understand and they become ineffective. The leader who leads must understand the culture, which comes from reading, listening, visiting, and observing. The leader learns to understand people by going where they work, visiting in their homes, sharing their joys and sorrows, and sticking close enough that leadership is not divorced from followship.[xcvi]

Lack of Christian commitment. Christian commitment is a total absolute for volunteers if quality service is to be provided. Where there is no intimacy with God, there is no commitment.[xcvii]

Enlistment of Volunteers for Training

Enlisting volunteers for the LTM is a necessary fete. It must be done as an encouragement and screening

process. It must take into consideration why people desire to volunteer and the proper method by which to enlist them for training. Persons serve in volunteer church positions for many reasons. In fact, it is seldom that a single reason provides the motivation for a person's service. More often, a combination of motives, some perhaps more noble than others, forms the basis for accepting and carrying out a church job.[xcviii]

Paul Veith, as cited in Reginald M. McDonough, *Working with Volunteer Leaders in the Church,* a noted author in the field of religious education, lists a variety of motivators for volunteer service.

There are, no doubt, many reasons which motivate people to render volunteer service—some high, some low. It seems, however, that adequate motivation for service in Christian education is that of the need and the opportunity, which should make an adequate appeal to every loyal church member. This major motivation may be supplemented by such things as a wholesome fellowship of the workers in Christian education, recognition on the part of the church, provision for attractive working conditions, a dignified and personal invitation from the church, indicating the ground on which this particular individual has been chosen.[xcix]

A brief explanation of some of the motives and needs that prompt persons to accept a volunteer church position will be given in the following paragraphs.[c]

To serve others. Service to fellowman is a central theme in Christianity. Service gives a person a way to put his concern into action.[ci]

To gain love and acceptance. Persons also accept volunteer positions because of their need to be accepted and loved by other persons. This need to belong is a normal social desire that exists in every healthy person. It is certainly not wrong to want to be involved in a group that can accept you as a person of worth, share your concerns, and help you weather the anxieties and frustrations of life.

The relationship of belonging to the need to participate in volunteer service is explained this way. Volunteer service answers the need to belong that each of us has—the need to become associated with others in achieving some tangible goal. In many jobs a man works on a part of something, or is a "specialist" in something. He may never see the whole job or the completed job. He feels the need to belong to a group of people with similar interests to accomplish something he can see, to achieve satisfaction in a completed job. Volunteer service can be an answer to this need. For women, too, volunteer service helps to answer the need to belong to some group outside the family. Many women whose children are grown find volunteer work an antidote to feelings of emptiness and loneliness.[cii]

Unfortunately, the need to belong to a group can become a dominating need in a person's life and cause him to accept responsibilities for which he is not capable. A person feels that their friends will reject them if they do not say yes.[ciii]

To obtain recognition and status. The fact that some persons accept church leadership position to achieve recognition and status is both good and bad. It is good because God has placed within each person the gifts that he expects to be used. To desire a platform for the stewardship of these gifts is commendable. A person with the gift of teaching should have a desire for a position in which he can use the gift for the Lord.[civ]

On the other hand, a person who accepts a position to advance their status or power in the church or community is doing themselves and the church a great disservice. It is this type of hypocrisy that makes a church suspect to persons in the community who see through the sham.[cv]

Other persons accept church leadership position because of their deep-felt need for recognition. In many instances, recognition may not be possible for them in other areas of their lives. They may be starving for someone to say, "Well done." The ministry of affirmation is a significant responsibility for every leader.[cvi]

To find self-fulfillment. Accepting a church leadership position to obtain a sense of accomplishment from achieving a short- or long-term goal is a highly desirable motive. A person who has self-fulfillment as a motive obtains satisfaction from putting into practice the talents and skills he possesses. Persons who serve because of this motive might say: "God has given me a gift to teach. It is a thrilling experience for me. I love to see people grow." Fortunately, there are many church leaders who sincerely feel this way. They have a sense of mission about their work. Rather than service being a burden, it is a joy.[cvii]

To serve God. Service to God is vital to everyone who feels a debt of gratitude for God's work in his or her life. This overwhelming motivation cuts across the other reasons that have been given. To see a position as an opportunity for influence is a service to God. And certainly, to fulfill a divine mission is to serve God. The apostle Paul said, "I press toward the mark for the prize of the high calling"; "the love of Christ constraineth us."[cviii] Every Christian is grateful to God for his love and redemption. Belonging, recognition, status, and fulfillment needs are God-given. God can work through these needs to lead individuals to accept and faithfully carry out his will.[cix]

Without the consideration of the aforementioned reasons why volunteers volunteer for service, the enlistment process would be severely handicapped. However, with the information one can appeal to these needs as a springboard for enlisting volunteers for service. It is also necessary to build the worker up by providing training in the area where the training will please God and edify the worker.

The process of enlistment should be well planned. It should begin with a study of the leadership needs of a church. The study should be two-fold. First, determine the present and future priorities the church must establish to achieve its mission. Leadership is one of only four resources—leaders, time, money, and facilities—that a church has to do its work. Leadership should be placed according to the priority mission of the church.[cx]

Second, the study should be a forecast of leadership needs. This forecast is based on the present organizational structure; however, it should reflect changes in the structure that are projected because of anticipated program and enrollment changes. It should pinpoint the number and types of leaders that will be needed at the beginning of each of the next three years. The forecast will serve as a basis for designing the church's pre-service training plan.[cxi]

Determining Leadership Needs

In deciding leadership needs, there are seven steps used to make the determination. Initially, a decision must be made regarding a desirable leader/pupil ratio. As an example, one to ten can be used as an across-the-board figure, but for the forecast it will be more helpful to select a specific figure for each age group. Secondly, calculate the present needs. Check the present leader/pupil ratio. There may be some areas where we are not presently meeting our expectation. Thirdly, project the enrollment for at least the next three years. To do this accurately, examine at least three sources: the growth or decline of the various groups in recent years, community trends, and church plans for strategic advance. The fourth step is to figure

83

the number of leaders that will be needed to staff each year's enrollment. The fifth step consists of checking the turnover. Turnover is a major factor of leadership forecasting. Step six is designed to put it all together. The last step in developing the forecast is the act of thinking through the type of leaders that will be needed.[cxii]

It is the author's conviction that the leadership skills needed to accomplish a church's mission can be found within its membership. This is a difficult conviction to live by because I know of no church that has all the leaders it could use effectively. But God will not give a mission if the resources are not available to accomplish it. The challenge is to discover the gifts and other resources God has placed in the membership and link them together effectively.[cxiii] The first step of an enlistment process is to set up a discovery system that will facilitate a match-up of the gifts and interests of persons with the leadership needs of the church's program.[cxiv]

Investigate Multiple Sources

Locating church members with the skills and interests needed to fill positions is hard work. The most frequent shortcoming of a minister or nominating committee is to consider only persons who come to mind. It is amazing how many persons will be overlooked by making a list through a series of mental gymnastics only.

Many sources can and should be used to find potential leaders. There are possibilities for locating leaders in the church roll, adult and older youth in church training, vacation Bible school faculty, new church members, returning college students, returning servicemen and women. Persons attending conferences and conventions, associated officers and substitute teachers, persons who have completed training courses and persons included in talent files provide good sources for possible leadership candidates. Of course, school teachers and administrators, businessmen and women whose work requires group leadership, retired persons, church members who are leaders in community affairs, and persons who have previously served as teachers and officers should be given special consideration. Often overlooked potential leaders can be discovered on information letters of recommendation from other churches, potential leader classes, recommendation from present teachers and officers, recommendation from deacons regarding their membership groups, and visitation contacts. [cxv]

After a list of potential leaders has been developed, then we come to the crucial task of selecting the persons to be contacted, making the contact and securing a commitment to serve.[cxvi]

In past efforts to enlist persons for leadership training, potential volunteers were not approached properly and information relative to the needs of the church, personal qualifications, and leadership training goals were not disclosed. Therefore, to enhance a greater possibility of participation, a proper atmosphere for enlisting prospects must be developed.

Some Christians may feel like babes in Christ and unworthy to hold a leadership position. Others may fail to see the wide variety of leadership opportunities that are available. Other Christians may not be serving because of sin in their lives. They know the needs and have ability but will not respond because of the cost of discipleship. Some persons may not respond because they simply are not aware of the needs. Some persons hesitate because of a lack of self-confidence. These persons need assurance and training. Some are not serving because they have not been asked.cxvii

Regardless of the reason, it is helpful to seek to build a climate in which the Holy Spirit can guide a person to consider his gifts and consecrate them to service. Many methods can be used such as sermons, bulletin boards, dedication services, articles in the church newsletter, special programs in departmental events, studies in Sunday school and church membership training.cxviii

There needs to be established a positive climate for leadership. Through a major research study, the leadership has learned some of the factors, which are present in strong, vital alive congregations. The four factors which have been identified, along with three others to be noted, are valuable pieces of information. They enlighten our understanding of what healthy church life is like. They increase our insight into the particular areas of church life, which we can work to strengthen.[cxix]

Cohesiveness. Healthy vital churches demonstrate a high degree of cohesion. Cohesiveness in a group or organization is difficult to define. Cohesion has been called the social glue that holds a group together. Membership means a great deal to persons involved in a highly cohesive church. They are willing to put their involvement in the church at top priority.[cxx]

Mutual support. Healthy vital churches report an awareness of mutual support. They know they are part of a team, each concerned about the wellbeing of the other. Support permeates the fabric of their relationship network as an ongoing process. They understand that they are accountable to one another; yet, they have confidence that when they are having trouble doing all that they are supposed to do, there are others who will walk alongside or even move in and carry the entire load.[cxxi]

Efficiency. Healthy, vital churches work with efficiency. They put their decision-making, their planning, and their programming involvements together in ways that maximize the use of persons' energies and minimize their use of time. They are

88

willing to come together and accomplish little or to drift along with no forethought given to direction of process.[cxxii]

Adaptability. Finally, healthy, vital churches sense the need and move ahead to adapt to change. The

content of our faith remains the same, but the manner in which it is applied to our ways of being the church and to our personal lives has to change. If we refuse to change or become paralyzed by the need to change, in a sense we contribute to distorting the meaning of our faith in our day.

The Spirit's presence. Vital, healthy, growing churches inevitably seem to have a renewed sense that the Spirit of God is moving in their midst, leading them to take risks to be what and where God wants them to be.[cxxiii]

Small groups. Churches which are experiencing renewed vitality nearly always have incorporated a significant small group ministry of some kind into their fellowship. A depth of sharing and a commitment to care for one another in concrete ways is to build into the fabric of the group experience. There seem to be many patterns which can work to accomplish a small group ministry. The best way is the one which most adequately meets the needs of a specific congregation.[cxxiv]

Leadership core. A central core of concerned committed leaders can usually be identified in vital, healthy churches. They are persons who give of themselves in dedicated ways to seek direction, to initiate some movement, to enlist others, to ensure ongoing involvement.[cxxv]

To the degree that congregations are vital and healthy, leadership recruitment becomes easier. Working to increase the vitality of congregational life contributes to securing and maintaining a solid leadership structure.[cxxvi]

Barriers to Leadership Recruitment

Unfortunately, even congregations with a great deal of vitality discover there are barriers to overcome in securing leaders. These barriers have to be acknowledged, understood, and addressed.[cxxvii]

Time. Our environment is one in which many people find that time is their most precious life resource. There are not enough hours in the week to do what they have to do, are expected to do, or want to do. There are numerous activities that they would enjoy and believe in; but they have only a limited amount of time available.[cxxviii]

Pluralism. Setting priorities in a pluralistic environment where there is such a smorgasbord of options is a monumental challenge. The choices are difficult because of the ambiguity which seems to permeate the process of choosing alternatives. [cxxix]

Structure. For some persons, the structure of their lives is such that involvement in church leadership seems futile—particularly if they want to be regular in attendance and to contribute beyond the minimum expectation.[cxxx]

Depletion. More persons are involved in service jobs than ever before in history. Many of them find that they are constantly being asked to direct their life energy flow toward meeting the needs of others. They simply feel they "can't give any more," even though the opportunities sound worthwhile.[cxxxi]

Low self-worth. Some persons hesitate to accept the invitation to involvement in leadership because they struggle with pervasive feelings of low self-worth. They simply do not believe that they have anything to contribute that someone else cannot do substantially better. An observer may think there often appears to be no reality base to the self-worth struggles of a person who seems to be talented, attractive, and gracious in approach to others. But judgments about the self are deep internal evaluations growing from early life experiences. An "outsider" may not find such an assessment accurate, but it is likely to be firmly anchored in the belief system of the person who concludes, "I am not good enough to be a follower. "If people knew me, I am not even good enough to belong to this church. I won't get involved."[cxxxii]

The Value of Self-Worth

Being a victim of racism and various forms of deprivation such as poverty, broken home, and illiteracy, I believe one's self-worth is called into question when challenged to rise above one's normal state of existence. Personally, I have devalued myself due to internal and external influences such as those mentioned. In addition, I certainly believe racism has robbed many ethnic groups of a degree of their self-worth and self-esteem.

As the author has stated, an outsider may not understand the stripping of one's personhood through racism and impoverishment, but I firmly suggest, due to my firsthand experience, it has done something to the deprived in our society. Therefore, in developing an LTM for the Eastern Star, a church whose membership is comprised primarily of people of deprivation, special measures must be taken to provide a curriculum that will deal with their needs, which will meet them where they are, boost their self-worth, and enlist them for volunteer service.

If every gift is to be used in the church, persons of low self-esteem must by God's design, and necessity for proper church function, be drawn into a training program, trained however long it takes, and provided opportunity to participate in the workforce of God's kingdom and His church; thus, perpetuating the procedure of equipping saints for the work of the ministry and increasing the workforce.

Through my experience as a pastor, those persons who have developed a renewed perception of themselves through special time and interest invested in them, have demonstrated a high degree of commitment to Christ. This is symbolic of Mary Magdalene who Jesus showed much interest after having a low self-worth (Mark 16:9).

Leadership recruitment for the church has to occur within the realities of modern life with all the barriers it presents. Time, a plurality of opportunities, restrictions from structure, depletion from continual service to others, and the questioning of self-worth—all present barriers to a positive response when persons are asked to accept the challenge to become involved in strategic leadership processes in the church.[cxxxiii] During a banquet speech Dr. Lincoln N. Bingham stated, "All churches are not conducive of producing the same fruits."[cxxxiv]He then encouraged all pastors to consider the soil (location and demographics) of the church and community where one pastors. That statement has stayed with me to this very day. Often, I question God and myself as to whether I am asking for too great a yield from the resources which God has endowed Eastern Star. In addition, I am jokingly reminded of my undying efforts to raise the standard by a church deacon, Joe Thomas, who always says to me, "The reason Rome wasn't built in a day was because you were not the supervisor."[cxxxv] I take that as compliment because it expresses my unending commitment and desire to raise the standard and please God.

The Bible teaches, "All things are possible with God." As a result of my firm belief in God, I serve with the idea in mind, though Eastern Star may not have the financial resources to hire an administrative staff, his church can still reach its potential because God has gifted it with members who have what is needed to perform God's cause and mission on earth. Therefore, the challenge is to discover, enlist, and train existing potential leaders in the church.

Conclusion

The content of chapter three helps the troubling spirit in my soul to find a way to overcome Satan's attacks on would be servants of God through apathy, complacency, excuse, lack of knowledge and low self-worth. The church, the body of Christ, has many members, and not all members have the same function. Therefore, it is absolutely disturbing to a pastor/leader to have non-enlisted and non-functioning potential leaders and members. It is disheartening because the body, in order to operate at its fullest potential, must employ every gift for service. Otherwise, where there is idleness, the devil's ideas will prevail. So, to offset Satan's endeavors to impede God's work, potential leaders must be sought and trained to equip others for the work of the ministry.

CHAPTER 4

NEEDS ASSESSMENT QUESTIONNAIRE

In an effort to determine the needs of paid staff, active volunteers, those responding due to the enlistment process, and potential volunteers, a pretest was developed.

Leadership Training Model

The questionnaire was designed to gather pertinent information from each participant for the development of an LTM. The questionnaire was administered to persons who were interested in leadership training and agreed to participate. Along with Eastern Star, three other churches were tested. The purpose of including other churches was to gather information from diverse volunteers to broaden the database regarding volunteer leadership needs. The participants were male and female ranging in ages thirteen and up. This research instrument is designed, not only for the purpose of discovering existing qualities, possible deterrents to volunteering for service, but also to reveal areas of need that hinder competent leadership in the Eastern Star.[cxxxvi]

Session I: The Purpose of God in Salvation

Goal. The intent of this teaching session was to familiarize participants with God's purpose in the redemptive work of the Lord Jesus. It was designed to dispel the deception that believers are not required to do anything after receiving God's unspeakable gift of salvation. Therefore, the desired outcome of this session was that of facilitating behavior change in existing leaders, volunteers, and potential leaders so they would make the proper response for the blessing of the free gift of salvation.

Objectives. The objectives to be utilized in accomplishing the aforementioned goal will be that of explaining God's purpose in salvation. Second Corinthians 5:19 will be used as the basic scripture foundation for providing understanding of God's purpose in salvation. That passage of scripture states . . . "that God was in Christ, reconciling the world unto himself, not imputing their trespasses unto them; and hath committed unto us the word of reconciliation."

The second objective will seek to make plain the process of salvation. It is necessary to do so to dispel the idea that we can earn our salvation. Therefore, Ephesians 2:8-9 will be used as the scriptural reference. The passage makes this declaration, "For by grace are ye saved through faith; and not that of yourselves: it is the gift of God: not of works, lest any man should boast." Within this teaching objective, the grace of God will be defined as well as believing faith that, in this instance, activates God's grace in the redemptive act of God.

The third objective endeavors to make plain how one should respond to salvation though it is the free gift of God. According to Romans 12:1-2, there is a proper mode of response. Paul teaches this manner of response through the words of that scripture text, "I beseech you therefore, brethren, by the mercies of God, that ye present your bodies a living sacrifice, holy, acceptable unto God, which is your reasonable service. And be not conformed to this world: but be ye transformed by the renewing of your mind, that ye may prove what is that good and acceptable, and perfect will of God." This explanation will create within the participants an awareness of the status or relationship with God and internally encourage a response.

The fourth and final objective sheds light on the product of one's salvational relationship with God. The relationship is the end result of accepting Jesus Christ as savior through faith and endeavoring to honor His will through carrying our His purpose in our lives.

This is to be done in compliance to God's purpose in the recipient's life. Because Ephesians 2:10 teaches, "For we are his workmanship, created in Christ Jesus unto good works, which God hath before ordained that we should walk in them."

Concluding the session. At the conclusion of this session, the participants should have a thorough understanding of God's purpose in salvation. They should realize now, though salvation is a free act of God, it does call for a personal response from all that it has been bestowed upon. Further, they should know the origin, purpose, process, and by product of salvation. And finally, they should realize the call of God through salvation is not a call to idleness, but a call to committed service.

Teaching technique. The primary teaching technique utilized will be the lecture method. However, at the beginning of the session, the class will be divided into small groups. Each group will be given a relative question to God's purpose in salvation that will invite group interaction and gather information that each group will share with the class. These questions seek to make determination on individual understanding on God's purpose in salvation. This information will be used during the session as class dialogue information. Also, at the end of each session, research assignments will be made to enhance the participant's knowledge base.

Teaching tools. The Bible will serve as the fundamental resource tool. The overhead projector will aid in providing a backdrop for the transparencies that give significance to the teaching content of the session. The transparencies for sessions can be found in the appendixes.[cxxxvii]

Session II: Discovering Your Spiritual Gifts

Goal. Session II is designed to make known to participants that God has endowed them with the necessary gifts to fulfill His assigned purpose in their lives. Included in this goal is teaching that will enlighten volunteers on the false assumption that only certain Christians have spiritual gifts. It will explain where spiritual gifts originate, when they are bestowed upon a believer, types of gifts, and their specific purpose. The biblical foundation is 1 Corinthians 12:1-12 and Colossians 2:10.

Objectives. The first objective in realizing the goal of discovering one's spiritual gift(s) is to administer a test (see Appendix two) for leadership potential. This test is designed to determine leadership potential that one may have that is latent due to a lack of use. This lack of use may be due to lack of opportunity, the thought that one does not have a gift(s) or, simply complacency. However, the leadership test will reveal the possible leadership gifts many may have.

The second objective is to explain the role of gifts in the church. Included in this effort will be that of the distinguishing spiritual gifts from fruits of the spirit. Also, gifts will be distinguished from talents (natural abilities). Gifts will be categorized into specific groups for use in various ministries. With this knowledge, each one will realize how important spiritual gifts are to the church, the body of Christ, and how necessary it is for each gift to function according to its role in the church.

The third objective is to lead volunteers to discover their gift(s). This is absolutely necessary because many believers have no knowledge of the wealth God has given His church through them in the form of spiritual endowments. Yet, the greater portion

of would-be servants never use them. Therefore, they die, taking their untapped potential to the graveyard with them. Hence, seven suggestions will be made to help volunteers discover their spiritual gifts. They are Delineation: list the gifts; Doing of service: go to work; Desire: note your inclination; Dedication; Development; Delight; and Discernment by others.

The fourth objective is to encourage volunteers to utilize their spiritual gifts in service for the cause and kingdom of God. Creating an opportunity to serve will bring on this encouragement and teaching that will enlighten on the penalty for not using and rewards for using ones God given gifts. This teaching will heighten their understanding of their personal involvement in the purpose and function of the church.

Concluding the session. At the conclusion of this session, all will have a better understanding of their potential of leadership as revealed by the leadership potential test. They will have a thorough understanding of the role of gifts in the church, have knowledge of how to further discover their God given gifts, and having that knowledge, they should be encouraged to seek opportunity to use their gifts for the advancement of God's work.

Teaching technique. The teaching technique for this session will be comprised of small group participation. Each group will be assigned questions for discussion and will report on them before class lecture takes place. In this session, the leadership potential test will be done in a group with each person answering according to how they rate, then sharing with the group, and finally with the entire class from a group perspective. After that has been completed, the lecture or dialogue method will begin.

This will be the technique throughout, except for periods of questions and answers.

Teaching tools. As teaching tools, the Bible will be referred to throughout the session. As a matter of fact, other passages of scripture will be dealt with to further substantiate the interpretation of another passage of scripture. Also, as visual aids, transparencies of complementary information on the subject of Discovering Spiritual Gifts will be used to enhance comprehension.

Session III: The Attitude of Leadership

Goal. The goal of this session is to develop a deeper understanding of the leadership style of Jesus. The participants will be brought into the knowledge that Jesus' ideology on leadership is quite different from that of the world. Leadership in the kingdom of God will be differentiated from the worldly concept of leadership. Therefore, it will be made clear that kingdom leaders are people who lead like Jesus. The Biblical foundation is Matthew 20:25-26; Mark 10:45; and Philippians 2:5-11.

Objectives. The first objective will be that of defining servant leadership. This definition is derived from the words of Jesus as recorded in Matthew 20:25, 26. Therein it is stated, "But Jesus called them unto Him, and said, ye know that the princes of the Gentiles exercise dominion over them, and they that are great exercise authority upon them. But it shall not be so among you: but whosoever will be great among you, let him be your minister."

The second objective is to study the biblical concept of servant leadership. This study will include various examples of servant leadership as displayed by Jesus. It will familiarize volunteers with the attitude of Jesus in service as God works in and through His life. Also, other scriptural references will be used to magnify the divine intent of God in Jesus Christ manifest in Jesus' servant spirit.

The third objective has as its focus that of emphasizing the humility of Jesus in service. The essence of this is Mark 9:35b. The message of this passage is this: ". . . if anyone wants to be first, he must be the very last, and servant of all."

The fourth objective will discuss the attitude of leadership prevalent today. It will shed light on this generation's emphasis on power, position, prestige, and titles. This effort in teaching will reveal to the participants the question, "Who is number one?" has crept into the Christian ranks.

The fifth objective highlights Philippians 2:5-11. The passage states, "Let this mind be in you, which was also in Christ Jesus: Who, being in the form of God, thought it not robbery to be equal with God: But made himself of no reputation, and took upon him the form of a servant, and was made in the likeness of men: And being found in fashion as a man, he humbled himself, and became obedient unto death, even the death of the cross. Wherefore God also hath highly exalted him, and given him a name which is above every name: That at the name of Jesus every knee should bow, of things in heaven, and things in earth, and things under the earth; And that every tongue should confess that Jesus Christ is Lord, to the glory of God the Father." Its sole purpose is to expose the intimate relationship Jesus had with his Father, and the extent to which He went to please Him and the sacrifice He made to redeem fallen humanity back to God.

The last objective will be that of discussing the seven principles of leadership. Within these principles is teaching on humility, seeking position and power, greatness in service, risk taking to serve others, taking up Jesus' towel of servant hood, sharing responsibility and authority, and multiplying leadership by empowering others. All of these principles were at work in and through Jesus as He worked out God's will in His life.

Concluding the session. When this session is completed, participants should know Jesus approach to leadership was a direct expression of His relationship with God, His father, and His internal condition (attitude) which he manifested in the way He honored God through serving others. The knowledge of how Jesus ministered should foster a different approach on the part of those who participated in the training session. And, above all, everyone should know service in God's kingdom is different from that practiced in the world.

Teaching technique. The lecture/dialogue will be the approach to conveying the content.

 However, small group discussion and class participation will be used. Also, since this session is personal and intimately related to interacting with others, intimate exercises will be utilized to make the content come alive. Also, personal research assignments will be given when necessary.

Teaching tools. The teaching tools consist of the Bible, pen and paper, overhead projector, and visual aids that highlight certain issues and subjects that enhance the teaching learning process. Though they are listed as they are, they all may not be used because other dynamics may enter the teaching process that necessitates using one or none of the above mentioned tools. The teaching aids included by design but not by necessity.

Session IV: The Needs and Process of Leadership

Goal. The purpose of this session is to identify the basic needs and general process of leadership, which will provide knowledge for volunteers and aid in their efforts to provide competent leadership. The acquisition of knowledge by participants will encourage the possibility of their volunteering for leadership positions in the church. Also, existing volunteers will be built up in their current fields of labor and possibly feel better qualified to provide a higher level of competency in leadership. The biblical foundation is Ephesians 4:11 and 1 Corinthians 14:40.

Objectives. The first objective is to provide fundamental teaching for volunteers in the areas of need as revealed in the survey results. The survey results revealed the following areas of need: self-esteem, relationship skills, communication skills, group building skills, conflict management, and time management. It was also revealed that training in the process of providing leadership was needed in the area of running meetings, principles of motivation, how to make an organization work, making assignments, leadership tasks, and job description. Though this objective appears to be cumbersome and difficult, it is absolutely necessary that these subjects be dealt with. Otherwise, volunteers will not benefit from the session which is designed to build leadership competency in volunteers and potential volunteers.

The second objective is that of familiarizing volunteers with basic leadership functions in the church. These functions consist of initiating, planning, organizing, inspiring, communicating, and providing directions for those who follow followers. However, there are other areas of needs that may dictate other leadership functions.

The third objective is to acquaint participants with job descriptions. This will aid in removing the excuse, "I would volunteer, but I don't know what to do." Job descriptions are necessary for building confidence in volunteers and would be volunteers. Without job descriptions, it would be comparable to the blind leading the blind.

The fourth objective is that of studying the eight law of leadership. These laws are relative to any form of leadership endeavor. If followed, they will serve as a sure foundation for developing good leadership practices in volunteers.

Teaching technique. The lecture/dialogue method will be the style of teaching used. A greater emphasis will be placed on displaying transparencies on the overhead. Also, personal leadership endeavors and encounters will be discussed to determine what impact prior leadership training may have made on their leadership assignments.

Teaching tools. The Bible, overhead projector, transparencies, and handouts will be the general teaching tools. They will be utilized based on subject matter. Role play and skits will serve to press various leadership principles to understanding.

Session V: The Cost and Reward of Leadership

Goal. The desired result is to make volunteers aware of the inevitable cost and the rewards of leadership. This teaching session will inform participants of the reality of the rejection and resentment that may be incumbent upon those who would please God through exemplary leadership. It will seek to enable leaders to know and endure hardship as one of God's soldiers. Also, the session will inform participants of the rewards of leadership. The session is so designed so as to teach suffering as a means of Christian maturity and future reward. The biblical foundation for this session is Romans 12:1-2; Matthew 6:24, 39, 7:21, Revelation 2:10.

Objective. The first objective is to lead volunteers into an understanding of possible situations and circumstances that may confront them as they present themselves as sacrificial servants for leadership. This session will clearly define cost and reward to insure volunteers thoroughly understand the concept of Christian leadership. Its primary intent is to resolve doubt by providing illuminating teaching on the difficulty and rewards of service.

The second objective is to make volunteers cognizant of the blessings and favor of God on those who serve Him. It will be made clear, the most precious of all God's blessings is God's approval, Jesus' presence, and the leading and the comfort of the Holy Spirit. And it will also provide within the leader a sense of meaning and usefulness as a Christian.

The third objective is to lead volunteers in

committing themselves for service as volunteer leaders

 and overall Christian service. This will be in the form of a challenge. They will be challenged to put God first in their lives. A pledge to provide ongoing training and support will be made, and the invitation to commit themselves for in service training will be extended. And, finally, a commitment agreement will be signed.

Concluding the session. In concluding this session, I believe all will have been brought face to face with the cost and rewards of leadership. They will recognize the sacrifices that one must make to serve God. And, if they have not had any personal experience (cost and rewards of leadership), certainly they should have some understanding of what others encounter in their efforts to advance the cause and kingdom of God through sacrificial leadership.

Teaching tools. The Bible serves as the reference book. Handouts will be used as follow-up references. Also, information on transparencies will be made available to participants as needed.

Teaching technique. The teaching technique will be lecture/dialogue. Group discussion will be utilized as a means of class participation and responding to the lecture material in the form of small group reports. Each group will discuss an issue, come to an agreement on the issue in question, and make a report before the class.

Questionnaire Results

In reviewing the respondent's answers to the survey questions, thirty one stated they have been Christians for eleven years or more; six, six to ten years; three, two to five years; and one less than one year. Thirty-five acknowledged a volunteer as being one who is not paid for service. All had provided service as a volunteer except two. Their service tenure ranged in time from less than one year to fifteen years or more.

They listed, to please God as their number one reason for volunteering; a need to belong as their second, by request third, and self-fulfillment as their fourth. Those who listed "to please God" as their main purpose felt the need to respond to the blessings of God upon their lives, while others were influenced by outside, personal, and a combination of those dynamics and a desire to show gratitude to God, His church and their fellowman. Only two persons failed to answer.

After defining talents and spiritual gifts and answering the questions, thirty-six said they have talents and gifts which they could contribute as volunteer leaders in various ministries of the church that would edify the saints and advance the work of the church. The remaining participants were the younger persons. They felt they really had not discovered their gifts or determined whether they had gifts and talents at all.

The majority of those answering the question, how has your experience as a volunteer been, twenty-three checked rewarding, seventeen fulfilling, six difficult, and one disappointing. Many felt the quality of their service would have been of a better quality if prior training had been provided. The teaching/training needs were diverse in nature. They felt, based on their past struggles, failures and disappointments, their needs were in the areas of job history/knowledge, job requirements/job description, self-esteem, interpersonal skills, and communicative skills. The need for seminars and ongoing workshops were of high priority.

Self-perception, self-worth, concept and leadership process also received a glaring look based on volunteer leadership concern. They felt total inadequacy in these areas. Yet, they unequivocally felt volunteers could develop into outstanding servant leaders. As a matter of survey data, they felt volunteer work should not be of a lesser quality than that of paid or specialized service workers. However, when asked to rate their level of volunteer commitment, fourteen indicated they were totally committed, seventeen partially committed, nine half committed, and one said not committed.

The questions, do other races or ethnic groups provide a better quality of volunteer leadership; and do you feel racism has any bearing on volunteer leadership for minorities, are of great interest because many of the respondents thought they did.

Interviews

The choice of Carolyn Connor and Doris Cox to respond to the interview question, "do you feel racism has any bearing on volunteer leadership for minorities," was not without serious consideration. They were made choice of stemming from the fact that they had encountered racism while raising their children and in their professional occupations as teachers in our public school system. Because they are school teachers, I felt they would have a more significant amount of information regarding self-esteem when dealing with racism and its potential to destroy self-worth.

Therefore, the following responses are the

thoughts and feelings of Mrs. Connor and Mrs. Cox and not myself.

Carolyn Connor's Response

The headline on the cover of the *Lexington Herald* dated June 25, 2001 stated in bold black print, "Blacks Continue to Fall Behind White Students."[cxxxviii] These questions immediately arose in my mind: Is this information noteworthy of front-page headlines? What message does this send? What advantage is to be gained by knowing this information and to whose advantage is it? This is only one example of how our nation continues to contribute to the low self-esteem fostered in the minds of many African Americans today.

Self-esteem has been defined as one's perception of himself/herself relative to self-worth or merit. Many factors contribute to the development of positive or negative self-esteem. One element is certain, when individuals are able to experience success their self-esteem is heightened. Regardless of socioeconomic factors, education, cultural barriers, and prejudice events that promote confidence in one's ability helps to develop a positive self-image. This concept is very simplistic in nature, however, for the African American this simple concept can become quite complex.

To properly evaluate why the *Lexington Herald* headline read as it did, to understand why the incarceration rates of African Americans continue to soar, and to understand why the majority of us continue to live in poverty we have to understand the impact that slavery continues to play in our nation. The philosophy of breaking down the mind and body of the black man and creating a matriarchal family is at the root of the problem. Divide and conquer ideologies keep us from bonding together to pull the entire race up. Even though we have come a long way and opportunities for minorities have greatly increased, the practice of individual and institutional racism perpetuated in the fiber of our nation's method of operation continue to affect our progress as a race.

Many of the programs instituted for the purpose of helping African Americans have in fact had adverse effects. For example, AFDC created and fostered a dependency while destroying the principal of self-sufficiency. Another debatable issue is the impact of busing. Busing did provide the cultural diversity that desegregation demanded, but did busing Black students to White schools increase their sense of self-worth and pride? The media continues to play a vital role in the development of self-esteem by the constant production of the "Ghetto Mentality Film."

So, how do we address this issue of low self-esteem in our culture? We know how the problem has been perpetuated therefore the greatest action needs to be focused on goals for improvement. We must implement systems where at the earliest ages possible success can be experienced. As a race we have to become as educated as we can for knowledge brings empowerment. We have to create opportunities for learning, practicing, and refining skills. We need to exercise our political rights to speak out and act upon elements in our society that have negative influences on our culture. We have to work hard to involve our children in positive personality shaping environments. We have to diminish the, "I've got mine, you get yours!" attitude.

In summary, self-esteem greatly influences the depth of a person's accomplishments and contributions to society. We have continually work towards the goal of assisting the weak so that they too can become strong. It is like the little boy who was going up and down the beach picking up starfish and placing them back into the ocean. A man asked what he was doing and he replied, "I'm trying to save them." The man responded, "You can't save them all." The boy said, "Maybe not, but I just saved one."[cxxxix]

Doris Cox's Response

Racism has definitely influenced whether or not Blacks readily step up to the bat and volunteer in leadership positions. Black folk are descendants of traditionally hard-working people brought here for forced labor, stripped of their dignity, and made to ride on the back seats of wagons, buses, or whatever had a back seat. Before they were slaves, they were indentured servants along with thousands of whites who worked for a number of years and gained their freedom. Those who wrote the history books, magazines, and newspapers left out the accomplishments of Blacks in order to control the future. They still have many of our minds under control.

I remember traveling the highways as a child and not being permitted to go in and sit down in a restaurant and eat. I remember riding on the train and having to sit up all night and not being able to lay down in the Pullman cars to sleep. I also remember the White waiting room and the Black waiting room. I remember being chosen last for a seventh grade basketball team and classmates not wanting to share the same shower. If you are over forty, think about how many Black faces you saw in your history books as you grew up, how many Black faces you saw on TV or the newspaper or in magazines. Why was that? Blacks were present on Bunker Hill, at Valley Forge, and in the Old West. How could they be overlooked? Is it because the advancements of the past

122

have been changed in order to make you think less of yourself in the future.

No other group has suffered this total burden of discrimination that Black people have. Black folk are accepted as second-class citizens by all of those in governmental authority, and have seen that myth perpetuated for so long that we, ourselves, even believe it. It is ingrained in our very being.

Watch us walk around with our heads hung down, our pants sagging, slouching in our seats, using language that disrespects our own selves and is inappropriate for our place of worship.

We pull each other down, and talk about each other instead of being supportive and encouraging. We fall into the traps of those who do not want us to do well. Our low self-esteem is passed down from generation to generation. Many of our young people are not being encouraged to surpass what we accomplished. These same young people grow up and will not step up and step out because they have not been encouraged to do so and have not seen their family members do so. Therefore, the leadership in the church is being compromised because we have fallen into the trap of racism.[cxl]

Response to Connor and Cox

Though the issue of racism is often tied to many social problems unjustly, I agree that this does play a serious role in the development of minorities and the disenfranchised. The question of the effects of low self-esteem due to racial bias and deprivation due to it, is real. And speaking from personal experience, and information gathered by working with minorities as a supervisor, student, and teacher, racism has made a noticeable effect of those who undergo it. These effects can be observed in one's self perception, lack of significant accomplishments in life, and unwillingness to take advantage of available opportunities.

As an African American, I have experienced the aforementioned feelings. Though I was hindered somewhat by their affects. I was able to overcome them and grow from the experience. However, it was no easy task.

To deal with what I perceived to be a problem, I enrolled in training dealing with self-esteem, and aligned myself with positive people.

Moreover, it was my determination to succeed that prevailed when all else failed. Life must go on. Therefore, to dwell on racial issues and not strive to overcome them is to set one's self up for failure.

The question, does racism keep us from volunteering, was posed as a means of gathering information to develop training in the LTM to offset it. Its intent was not to blame, but that of seeking a remedy.

However, in the response, one can determine, racism can and may be a hindrance to volunteerism due to past conditions and lack of a feeling of adequacy and acceptance.

Conclusion

Nevertheless, I believe, at the acceptance of Jesus Christ, and during the process of allowing Him to become the Lord of the believer's life, there should be a new perception of one's self. And if that is true, then the issue of racism in volunteering for service to God should be overcome by one's gratitude for the gift of salvation. That is not to deny that some may not overcome it as rapidly as others. However, the Bible teaches, greater is

He that is in the believer, than he that is in the world.

Therefore, included in the LTM there must be instruction in self-esteem building, not just to offset the effects of racism, but for all revealed hindrances. Volunteering should be in direct response to the goodness of God upon the believer's life and all possible deterrents to do so ought to be alleviated as much as the LTM will allow.

As a result of the data gathered from the survey, the following LTM was developed for Eastern Star. The sessions were held on five consecutive Sundays at the church in the fellowship hall. The time was 5:00 p.m. to 7:30 p.m. The ages ranged from 13 and up with mostly females involved. The materials needed are: tables and chairs to accommodate the number in attendance, an overhead projector, portable screen, microphone, folders for all participants to keep their session information. The sessions were videotaped for later view or to be used if a session was missed. The method of teaching used was small group discussions, lecture method, presentations, visual aids and transparencies.

CHAPTER 5

EVALUATION OF THE LTM

Chapter Five will provide evaluation and analysis of the goals and objectives set forth through the original purpose of this project. The strengths presently possessed by volunteers will be posted. The list of needs will be laid out. The area of needs to be addressed will be listed. Determination will be made of the benefits that training sessions have provided. Follow-up training will be scheduled; new enlistment efforts will be made after training

Forty-two volunteers and potential volunteers participated in the LTM teaching sessions. After having completed the training model, an evaluation questionnaire was developed and given to evaluate the effectiveness of the LTM.[cxli] During the five training sessions, information was made available to them that addressed their needs as indicated in the needs questionnaire administered prior to curriculum preparation.

Analytical Reflection

To determine whether or not the desired goal was accomplished through the training model, an analytical reflection was done on each question and answer. Each question was addressed providing the data as revealed by the questionnaire.

Question one. There was solidarity of the participant's view on the design of the LTM. They agreed 100 percent that the goal of the training model was to strengthen volunteer leaders. They would by objective be strengthened in the areas of their revealed need. The plan encroached in the questionnaire which serves to formulate the Leadership Training Module.

Question two. Ninety-three percent felt the LTM was a highly successful training tool. They felt better equipped as a leader after completing the leadership training sessions. And potential volunteers stated they were more prone to volunteer after the training than ever before.

Question three. The LTM was not intended to be an end in itself. Therefore, overwhelming success was the end result, because sixty-seven percent answered yes to the question, "Do you need additional training?" This provides opportunity to develop and implement an ongoing training process at the request of the larger portion of the class. Only thirty one percent stated they didn't need additional training, while only two percent didn't respond at all.

Question four. In response to what areas of additional training needs were prevalent in the participants many were listed. Time management, self-discipline, dealing with difficult people were areas of personal desired training. And, in general, the request for training in the areas of encouraging class participation, spiritual gifts, and communication was also listed. These needs are common among all leaders and training in those areas can never be addressed thoroughly in any one training session.

Question five. To this question it was indicated, information relative to building self-esteem, developing mutuality among people are needs of great interest. Some of the participants indicated they didn't perceive themselves as having potential to be leaders.

Others stated, they didn't think they would be well received. And others said they didn't have leadership gifts or talents.

Question six. The answers to this question showed a more than expected favorable appreciation for the content of the LTM and the instructor. Of the many encouraging statements made, declaring the training effort to be thorough, inspirational, and very helpful spoke well of the intent inherent training model's goal. The instructor, likewise, was deemed to be very well prepared, and very in-depth in presenting the content. However, it was stated time restraints on presenting the material forced the instructor to move swiftly through the session and the information presented.

Question seven. In presenting each session of the LTM, I was pushed due to my time limitation of two hours. However, all the sessions exceeded it. As a matter of fact several participants voiced their concern during the session. This was a clear indication they desired a clear and thorough understanding of the content. The teaching content was of great significance to them. So, in the final analysis of evaluating the time in which the modules were presented, ninety percent specified they did have ample time to complete the program.

Question eight. The question provides the most intimate and personal results for evaluating the training benefits of the LTM. Based on the critique of those who answered the questions, the LTM met their personal needs and confirmed many of their longtime beliefs regarding leadership principles and practices. They acknowledged being made aware of the cost and rewards of leadership, develop a positive view on volunteerism, a developed willingness to volunteer. All these positive responses were credited to the LTM. The teaching made them aware of their weaknesses and strengths and provided training to alleviate them. It was also stated by some, they gain a clear understanding of God's will for their lives. And more interesting, potential volunteers learned the need and necessity of commitment, and the zeal to do more for Christ was aroused.

Question nine. This question was answered in this manner, develop a method of enlistment that appeals to the entire body of volunteers. This method should be developed based on the needs of church and volunteers. It will begin at the inception of a member in the church, taught in the new member's class and under girded by ongoing training.

These questions will consist of job assignment and expectation. This will be a mandatory required class for all leaders and potential leaders, which will have as its motivating influence for completion needs related information and enthusiastic teaching.

Question ten. The last question of the gives a  well-rounded account of the total benefit of the LTM. The results seem to indicate the basic needs of those who desire to lead others but lack proper training. The findings revealed a gain in self-worth, which is of utmost importance in leadership endeavors. Because how one perceives themselves affects how one performs one's task. Structure in leadership efforts, knowledge about goal setting, the importance of job descriptions, knowledge of leaders should conduct themselves, knowledge of the prerequisites for leadership further empowers existing leaders for service and gave potential volunteers a sense of readiness for volunteers service.

Participant's Analytical Reflections

The analytical reflection on the purpose, goal, process, and benefit of the training model is reflected in the following statements by participants who took a second look at the overall effort of the LTM. The reflection provides a very favorable analogy of the leadership equipping effort. They indicated the LTM was planned with deep thought and facts regarding leadership, and prepared and presented out of a heart of care and compassion for active volunteers and potential volunteers.

Those that responded stated the context was very informative, systematically organized, and thought provoking. They also felt it could have been more effective if more time was allotted and more class participation was allowed.

However, according to them, the goal was accomplished. Volunteers feel they have a better understanding of God's will for their lives, how to do it, and the proper manner of how to conduct themselves in the process of doing. Through the process of the training endeavors, participants commented they had learned more about God's purpose in salvation, how to discover their spiritual gifts, Jesus' style of leadership, and the cost and reward of leadership.

Evaluation of the Results

As designed, the questions was used to determine the needs of volunteers before and after the training model respectably. Responses to the questions in the questionnaire revealed the needs of volunteers that they felt were major hindrances to their volunteering and providing exemplary leadership.

The evaluation revealed an overwhelming approval of the content of the LTM. Their responses to the question, "In what ways did you experience personal growth from the program?" is evidence that it was a great success.

Insight Gained

The project has profoundly enhanced my knowledge and understanding of the biblical, theological and historical concept, and approach to enlisting, training, and utilizing volunteer leaders.

Prior to the project, I was troubled by the fact that I had been called to pastor a church in a fertile location and didn't have the finances to carry out the existing and future ministries and administrative functions of the church. Therefore, I was overloaded with work and over spent in my efforts to make up the difference in giving.

However, the project provided me with an opportunity to research the issues and dispel some of the preconceived ideas I had as to why the members of Eastern Star would not volunteer their time, talent, and treasure for the up-building of God's cause and kingdom on earth. It was my belief, past experiences of deprivation, limited accomplishments, and racism hinders believers from volunteering because of low self-esteem. My beliefs were confirmed by the questionnaire results of African American participants and by the interview responses of African American teachers who teach in an integrated school system.

But this project broadened my view and understanding of the stumbling blocks and deterrents dealt with by active and potential volunteers. And it provided me with a burning desire to involve every member of Eastern Star in active service for the promotion of God's work and reproduction of leadership.

Influence on Future Leadership Training

Though the LTM yielded outstanding result, I feel just a small amount of knowledge was imparted during the five two-hour sessions. Therefore, future leadership training will include this project plus other relevant information that will refresh volunteers on past teachings and provide new and innovative ways of equipping the membership for service.

This project has led me to firmly believe what a church needs to carry out the tasks of the church, God provided it in and through those who have embraced Him through the Lord Jesus Christ. Therefore, it is God's will that every member and spiritual gift be actively pursued and enlisted in the workforce of the church. And that calls for an ongoing training program to prepare volunteers for service.

Knowing black people have had a past of devastating and debilitating experience with trying to maintain a sense of self-worth, future training dealing with the self-esteem will always be a vital part of leadership training for all leaders.

As a matter of fact, the issue of self-worth will be included in the new members study curriculum. This effort will be carried over into Bible study, various

136

seminars, and the ongoing leadership training program.

Moreover, future training will highlight commitment as the number one hindrance to volunteerism not racism. The level of one's commitment and gratitude should determine ones willingness to volunteer for service.

Conclusion

The development and implementation of the LTM for Eastern Star has been a monumentally successful task. But it will never reach its fullest intentions until it is implemented and used on an ongoing basis. The project places leadership training at the top of the list of hindrances for would be volunteers. If high priority is not placed on enlistment and training of volunteers, the current enthusiasm about leadership training will soon die.

As it stands at this point, the development and

implementation of the training model has satisfied my longing for a teaching tool that would encourage volunteerism in Eastern Star. I certainly feel the troubling in my soul has dissipated and will never rise to such levels as it was prior to this project endeavor.

I now believe, even stronger than before, everyone by virtue of God's unspeakable gift of salvation is a leader and has what it takes to do so. However, the gift must be cultivated through training and utilization.

After completing the Training Model, the church's volunteer leadership workforce has increased by fourteen persons. These persons have made public and private commitments to serve in positions of leadership. Each volunteer will be provided training prior training in the form of working with persons who hold positions of leadership which the volunteers desire to be trained.

Thus far, six of the fourteen currently have been trained and are providing leadership in the youth ministry, culinary department, children's church, church decoration, transportation, nursery, and education department. I believe the training provided through the Training Model has increased knowledge and made existing and would be volunteers feel better about themselves and created within them a desire to further God's cause and kingdom.

Having completed this Training Model, I feel a sense of great accomplishment. I also feel great things will be the final result of our endeavors from this point on in equipping the saints for the work of the ministry at the Eastern Star Baptist Church, 2400 Howard Street, Louisville, Kentucky. To God be the glory. A-men!

EQUIPPING VOLUNTEERS
FOR SERVICE

The Foundation for the Development of a Leadership Training Model

"And it came to pass on the morrow, that Moses sat to judge the people: and the people stood by Moses from the morning unto the evening. And when Moses' father-in-law saw all that he did to the people, he said, what is this thing that thou doest to the people? Why sittest thou thyself alone, and all the people stand by thee from morning unto even? And Moses said unto his father-in-law, because the people come unto me to inquire of God: When they have a matter, they come unto me; and I judge between one and another, and I do make them know the statures of God, and his laws. And Moses'

father-in-law said unto him, the thing that thou doest is not good. Thou wilt surely wear away, both thou, and this people that is with thee: for this thing is too heavy for thee: Thou art not able to perform it thyself alone. Hearken now unto my voice, I will give thee counsel, and God shall be with thee: Be thou for the people to Godward, that thou mayest bring the causes unto God. And thou shalt teach them ordinances and laws, and shalt show them the way wherein they must walk, and work that they must do. Moreover thou shalt provide out all the people able men, such as fear God, men of truth, hating covetousness; and place such over them, to be rulers of thousands, and rulers of hundreds, rulers of fifties, and rulers of ten. And let them judge the people at all seasons: and it shall be, that every great matter they shall bring unto thee, but every small matter they shall judge: so shall it be easier for thyself, and they shall bear the burden with thee. If thou shalt do this thing, and God command thee so, then thou shalt be able to endure, and all this people shall also go to their place in peace. So Moses hearkened to the voice of his father-in-law, and did all that he had said. And Moses chose able men out of all Israel, and made them heads over the people, rulers of thousands, rulers of hundreds, rulers of fifties, and rulers of tens. And they judged the people at all seasons: the hard causes they brought unto Moses, but every small matter they judged themselves."

THE QUESTIONNAIRE

- How long have you been a Christian?

    ___ Less than one year;

    ___ 2-5 yrs

    ___ 6-10 yrs

    ___ 11 years or more

- Who is a volunteer?

    ___ one who is not paid to service

    ___ one who is paid for service

- How long have you served as a volunteer leader?

    ___ 0 - 1 yr.

    ___ 1-5 yrs

    ___ 6-10 yrs

    ___11 yrs. or more

- Why did you volunteer?

    ___ by request

    ___ for recognition

    ___ self-fulfillment

    ___ to please God

    ___ a need to belong

- Do you feel you have something to contribute as a volunteer leader?

  ___ yes

  ___ no

- How has your experience as a volunteer been?

  ___ rewarding

  ___ disappointing

  ___ difficult

  ___ fulfilling

- Do you feel the quality of your volunteer service would have been better if prior training had been provided?

  ___ yes

  ___ no

- What areas of teaching/training do you think should be included in a volunteer leadership curriculum study?

  ___ history/knowledge

  ___ self-esteem

  ___ seminars

  ___ interpersonal skills

  ___ communicatives

  ___ workshops (hands on)

145

- In what areas do you feel inadequate as a volunteer leader?

  ___ self-perception

  ___ knowledge

  ___ concept

  ___ process

  ___ interpersonal skills

  If others, please list

  _____, _____,

- Can persons be developed into leaders?

  ___ yes

  ___ no

- Do other races/nationalities provide a better quality of volunteer leadership?

  ___ yes

  ___ no

- Do you feel racism has any bearing on volunteer leadership for minorities?

  ___ yes

  ___ no

- Do you think all volunteers should be provided a job description?

  ___ yes

  ___ no

- Do you feel volunteer work should be of a lesser quality than paid or specialized service?

  ___ yes

  ___ no

- Using the four listed categories, check the one that best describes your level of volunteer commitment.

  ___ a. not committed

  ___ b. partially committed

  ___ c. half-committed

  ___ d. totally committed

- Do you work well with others?

  ___ yes

  ___ no

- List your age. _____

- List your gender. _____

- Marital status. _____

- List as many reasons as you can as to why more Christians don't volunteer their services that a training program could alleviate.

  _____

  _____

  _____

  _____

  _____

- What is your educational level?

  ___ Elementary School

  ___ Middle School

  ___ High School

  ___ College

- Do you have time to be a volunteer leader?

  ___ yes

  ___ no

- Do you lack self- confidence?

  ___ yes

  ___ no

- Do you feel a paid staff worker's job is more prestigious/important than a volunteer?

    ___ yes

    ___ no

- Would you encourage others to volunteer and take the leadership-training course?

    ___ yes

    ___ no

- Please provide a written explanation of your choice.

_____

_____

_____

_____

Session One

1. Salutation

2. Purpose
   A. In fulfillment of the requirement of a doctor of ministry in black church leadership

   B. I am required to do a dissertation on a theme of my greatest interest, that being, developing a leadership training model for the Eastern Star Baptist Church.

   C. The training model has been developed and today I will teach the first of five sessions which comprise the training model

3. Introduction

4. Divide into groups (assign question)

   A. Discuss question 15 minutes

   B. Return to main class assembly

   C. Each group will report on the findings

5. Begin the teaching session

   A. The foundation of the model (transparency)

6. Definition of leadership (transparency)

7. Display the leadership training model (explain outline)

8. The teaching outline (Note: Display definition of leadership, see page 23)

The Leadership Training Model

Session I: The Purpose of God In Salvation

Goal

To lead volunteers into an understanding of God's Call upon their lives and how they should respond

Objectives

A. explain God's purpose in salvation

B. explain the process of salvation

C. explain the appropriate response to salvation

Scripture Passages

A. Ephesians 2: 8

For by grace are ye saved through faith; and that not of yourselves: it is the gift of God:

B. Ephesians 2: 10

For we are his workmanship, created in Christ Jesus unto good works, which God hath before ordained that we should walk in them.

C. Romans 12: 1, 2

I beseech you therefore, brethren, by the mercies of God, that ye present your bodies a living sacrifice, holy, acceptable unto God, which is your reasonable service. And be not conformed to this world: but be ye transformed by the renewing of your mind, that ye may prove what is that good, and acceptable, and perfect, will of God.

Teaching technique

   a. Group discussion on assigned statements

   b. Class dialogue

   c. Lecture

   d. Personal/research assignments

Teaching tools

   a. Bible
   b. Overhead projector
   c. Visual aids
          1. Transparencies
          2. Statement strips
          3. Truth based on Ephesians 4
          4. Motivation for ministry

Group discussions

Session II. Discovering Your Spiritual Gifts

Goal

To make known to volunteers, God has endowed them with the gifts to fulfill His assigned purpose in their lives.

Objectives

A. Administer a test for leadership potential

B. Explain the role of gifts in the church

C. Lead volunteers in an effort to discover their God-given gifts

D. Encourage volunteers to utilize their gifts

Scripture Passages

1 Corinthians 12:1-12

1 Now concerning spiritual gifts, brethren, I would not have you ignorant.

2 Ye know that ye were Gentiles, carried away unto these dumb idols, even as ye were led.

3 Wherefore I give you to understand, that no man speaking by the Spirit of God calleth Jesus accursed: and that no man can say that Jesus is the Lord, but by the Holy Ghost.

4 Now there are diversities of gifts, but the same Spirit.

5 And there are differences of administrations, but the same Lord.

6 And there are diversities of operations, but it is the same God which worketh all in all.

7 But the manifestation of the Spirit is given to every man to profit withal.

8 For to one is given by the Spirit the word of wisdom; to another the word of knowledge by the same Spirit;

9 To another faith by the same Spirit; to another the gifts of healing by the same Spirit;

10 To another the working of miracles; to another prophecy; to another discerning of spirits; to another divers kinds of tongues; to another the interpretation of tongues:

11 But all these worketh that one and the selfsame Spirit, dividing to every man severally as he will.

12 For as the body is one, and hath many members, and all the members of that one body, being many, are one body: so also is Christ.

Colossians 2:10

And ye are complete in him, which is the head of all principality and power:

Teaching Technique

    A. Small Group Assignments & Group Report

    B. Lecture/Dialogue

    C. Personal Assessment Test

    D. Personal/Research Assignments

Teaching Tools

    A. Bible

    B. Overhead Projector

    C. Visual Aids

        1. Transparencies

        2. Test for Leadership Potential

        3. What is Potential

Session III: The Attitude of Leadership

Introduction

Goal

> To familiarize volunteers with the Leadership Style of Jesus

Objectives

A. Define Servant Leadership

B. Study the Biblical concept of servant leadership

C. Examine Jesus' teaching on humility

D. Discuss the attitude of leadership prevalent today

E. Discuss the attitude of Jesus as demonstrated in Philippians 2: 5-11

F. List and discuss seven principles of servant leadership

Foundational Passages

Matthew 20: 25, 26

> 25 But Jesus called them unto him, and said, Ye know that the princes of the Gentiles exercise dominion over them, and they that are great exercise authority upon them.

26 But it shall not be so among you: but whosoever will be great among you, let him be your minister;

Mark 10: 45

45 For even the Son of man came not to be ministered unto, but to minister, and to give his life a ransom for many.

Philippians 2: 5-11

5 Let this mind be in you, which was also in Christ Jesus:

6 Who, being in the form of God, thought it not robbery to be equal with God:

7 But made himself of no reputation, and took upon him the form of a servant, and was made in the likeness of men:

8 And being found in fashion as a man, he humbled himself, and became obedient unto death, even the death of the cross.

9 Wherefore God also hath highly exalted him, and given him a name which is above every name:

10 That at the name of Jesus every knee should bow, of things in heaven, and things in earth, and things under the earth;

11 And that every tongue should confess that Jesus Christ is Lord, to the glory of God the Father.

Seven Principles of Servant Leadership

1. <u>Principle 1</u> Servant leaders humble themselves and wait for God to exalt them

2. <u>Principle 2</u> Servant leaders follow Jesus rather than seek a position

3. <u>Principle 3</u> Servant leaders give up personal rights to find greatness in service to others

4. <u>Principle 4</u> Servant leaders can risk serving others because they trust that God is in control of their lives

5. <u>Principle 5</u> Servant leaders take up Jesus' towel of servanthood to meet the needs of others

6. <u>Principle 6</u> Servant leaders share responsibility and authority with others to meet a greater need

7. <u>Principle 7</u> Servant leaders multiply their leadership by empowering others to lead

Leaders are teachers

(No one is unreachable if he/she is teachable–Terry Nance–God's Armor Bearers)

A. A leader takes care of his/her people

B. Leaders are faithful

C. Leaders pray in gratitude

D. Conclusion

E. Teaching Technique

1. Small group interaction

2. Group Reports

3. Lecture/Dialogue

4. Personal/Research Assignments

Teaching Tools

1.	Bible	3.	Overhead Projector
2.	Visual Aids	4.	Pen and Paper

Session IV. The Needs and Process of Leadership

Goal

To identify some of the basic needs and general process of leadership which will help volunteers to provide competent leadership.

Objectives

A. Provide fundamental teaching for volunteers in the areas of need as revealed in the survey

B. Familiarize volunteers with basic leadership functions in the church

C. Provide example of job descriptions

D. Display the OVERVIEW OF THE EIGHT LAWS OF LEADERSHIP on page 67 and explain

Areas of revealed needs training

1. self-esteem (self-worth)

2. relationship skills

3. communication skills

4. group building skills

5. conflict management

6. time management

Basic leadership functions

1. running meetings

2. principles on motivation

3. how to make organization work

4. making assignments

5. leadership tasks

Job descriptions

Overview: The Eight Laws of Leadership

Conclusion

Eastern Star Program against Guns and Gang Violence

Session V. The Cost and Reward of Leadership

Goal

> To inform volunteers of the possible cost and
>
> the rewards of leadership.

Objectives

1. to lead volunteers into an understanding of possible situations and circumstances that are incumbent upon those who serve God and others as volunteer leaders

2. to enlighten volunteers of the blessings of leadership

3. to lead volunteers in presenting themselves to Jesus Christ as volunteer leaders

Definitions

1. Cost

2. Reward

Foundational Passages

Romans 12: 1-2

> 1 I beseech you therefore, brethren, by the mercies of God, that ye present your bodies a living sacrifice, holy, acceptable unto God, which is your reasonable service.

2 And be not conformed to this world: but be ye transformed by the renewing of your mind, that ye may prove what is that good, and acceptable, and perfect, will of God.

Matthew 6: 24

24 No man can serve two masters: for either he will hate the one, and love the other; or else he will hold to the one, and despise the other. Ye cannot serve God and mammon.

Matthew 7: 21

21 Not every one that saith unto me, Lord, Lord, shall enter into the kingdom of heaven; but he that doeth the will of my Father which is in heaven.

Matthew 26: 39

39 And he went a little farther, and fell on his face, and prayed, saying, O my father, if it be possible, let this cup pass from me: nevertheless not as I will, but as thou wilt.

Revelation 2: 10

10 Fear none of those things which thou shalt suffer: behold, the devil shall cast some of you into prison, that ye may be tried; and ye shall have tribulation ten days: be thou faithful unto death, and I will give thee a crown of life.

Group Participation

1. Assign Group

    Each group will be assigned a passage of
    foundational scripture to discuss and
    report on regarding the cost and reward
    of leadership

    2. Class Reassemble

    Report on assigned passage giving their
    views of the text which unify it with the
    theme of the session, The Cost and
    Reward of Leadership

2. The Cost of Leadership

    The initial cost: Full Commitment

    The personal cost: Sacrifice

    The intangible cost: Dedication

    The tangible cost: Time

3. The Reward of Leadership

    1. Growth

        a. The way of growth is understanding others

        b. The leader must cultivate compassion

    2. Life enrichment

    3. Worthwhileness

4. Pay the price–receive the reward

5. Question and answer period

        Administer evaluation questionnaire

        Acknowledgment of graduation

        Final remarks and benediction

6. Teaching Tools

        Bible

        Discussion groups

        Overhead projector

      Visual Aids

        Eastern Star Program

Determining Results after the Teaching Sessions

Follow-up Questionnaire on the Leadership Training

Model for the Eastern Star Baptist Church.

1. Was the program designed to strengthen you as a volunteer leader?

_____ yes

_____ no

2 Do you feel better equipped as a leader?

_____ yes

_____.no

3. Do you need additional training?

_____ yes

_____ no

4. If so, in what areas?

_____

_____

_____

5. What could be added to the curriculum that was presented?

_____
_____
_____

6. How were the instructors?

_____
_____
_____

7. Did you have ample time to complete the program?

____ yes

____ no

8. In what ways did you experience personal growth from the training program.

_____
_____
_____
_____

9. What new enlistment procedure would you recommend for volunteer enlistment and training?

_____
_____
_____
_____

10. Do you feel others in the class benefited by the leadership training model?

Please list the ways in which they were.

_____
_____
_____
_____

EASTERN STAR POLICE AWARENESS EVENT

SESSION 1

THE PURPOSE OF GOD IN SALVATION

SMALL GROUP DISCUSSION

WHAT IS SATAN'S GREATEST DECEPTION(S) ABOUT OUR SALVATION?

The greatest deception which Satan, the enemy of our souls, has ever foisted upon humanity is the false but appealing doctrine that man can do something to earn his own salvation, by keeping the law of God.

The second greatest error is the teaching that we don't have to do anything after we are saved.

WHAT IS LEADERSHIP?

ACCORDING TO THE DICTIONARY, "TO LEAD" MEANS

📖 TO DRAW ALONG, GO AHEAD OR SHOW THE WAY

📖 TO MOVE BEFORE OR IN ADVANCE OF

📖 TO TAKE OR HAVE THE INITIATIVE

📖 TO MAKE A BEGINNING, GO OR ACT FIRST

📖 TO DIRECT AN ACTION, THOUGHT OR OPINION

📖 TO DRAW OR DIRECT BY INFLUENCE, GOOD OR BAD

STATEMENT STRIPS

1. EVERY CHRISTIAN IS A PRIEST.

2. GOD IS AT WORK APPROACHING THE BELIEVER.

3. THE BELIEVER HAS A RESPONSIBILITY TO SEEK OUT HIS/HER SPIRITUAL GIFT.

4. THE CHURCH HAS THE RESPONSIBILITY OF PROVIDING AN ADEQUATE PROGRAM FOR GIFT DISCOVERY.

5. THE CHURCH MUST AFFIRM OR NOT AFFIRM AN INDIVIDUAL BELIEVER'S CALL.

6. EVERY CHRISTIAN IS A MINISTER.

7. THE CALL TO SALVATION AND THE CALL TO MINISTRY ARE ONE AND THE SAME CALL.

8. THE PRIMARY RESPONSIBILITY FOR MINISTRY RESTS UPON THE SHOULDERS OF THE LAYPERSON.

MOTIVATION FOR MINISTRY

I.   GOD'S CALL IN THE CONVERSION EXPERIENCE

     A.   LIMITED UNDERSTANDING OF THE CONVERSION EXPERIENCE

     B.   DEEPER VIEW OF THE SALVATION RELATIONSHIP

     C.   NOT ENOUGH MINISTERS

II.   THE MEANING OF FAITH

     A.   FAITH – FUNDAMENTAL PART OF BEING SAVED

     B.   EXHORTATION RATHER THAN EXPLANATION

     C.   BIBLICAL PASSAGES ON SALVATION

     D.   REEXAMINATION OF CONVERSION EXPERIENCE

         1.   SALVATION IS GIFT

         2.   THE GIFT – IS IT CONDITIONAL OR UNCONDITIONAL?

AUTHENTIC FAITH

TRUTHS BASED ON EPHESIANS 4

1. THE MEANS OF EQUIPPING THE LOCAL BODY IS THROUGH THE LOCAL CHURCH.

2. EVERY BELIEVER IS A MINISTER.

3. BELIEVERS MUST BE EQUIPPED FOR MINISTRY.

4. THE PURPOSE FOR EQUIPPING IS TO PRODUCE GROWTH IN THE BODY OF BELIEVERS.

5. THE PASTOR HAS THE RESPONSIBILITY FOR PROVIDING THE GUIDANCE FOR GETTING BELIEVERS EQUIPPED

SESSION 2

DISCOVERING YOUR

SPIRITUAL GIFTS

GIFTS ARE NOT FRUIT

THE GIFTS OF THE SPIRIT DIFFER FROM THE
FRUIT OF THE SPIRIT IN MANY WAYS:

GIFTS	FRUIT
HAVE TO DO WITH SERVICE	HAVE TO DO WITH CHARACTER (LOVE, JOY, PEACE, ETC.; GAL 5: 22, 23)
ARE THE MEANS TO AN END	IS THE END (ROM 1: 11-13)
WHAT A MAN HAS	WHAT A MAN IS
GIVEN FROM WITHOUT IN PLURAL	PRODUCED FROM WITH OUT IN SINGULAR "BUT THE FRUIT"
ALL GIFTS NOT POSSESSED	EVERY VARIETY OF FRUIT SHOULD BE
BY EVERY BELIEVER	IN EVERY BELIEVER
WILL CEASE	PERMANENT (1 Corinthians 13:8-10 Living Bible)

- Possession of gifts does not indicate godliness of life.

- Samson continued to perform feats long after he was out of touch with God.

- Judas, likely one of the 70 who cast out demons, became a betrayer (Luke 10: 17).

- Two quarreling women at Philippi, whom Paul exhorted to make up, had previously exercised gifts with Paul (Phil. 4: 2, 3).

Gifts and Talents are Different

	TALENT	GIFT
Source:	Common grace of spirit	Special grace of spirit
Time given:	Present from natural birth	Present from new birth
Nature:	Natural ability	Spiritual endowment
Purpose:	Instruction, entertainment	Spiritual growth of saints
	Inspiration on a natural level	Christian service

📖 Talents and gifts are related.

📖 Literary, oratorical, artistic, musical, or linguistic talents may be avenues through which the Holy Spirit will use a person's gifts.

📖 But writing, speaking, or vocal abilities are talents, not gifts.

MINISTRY OF THE WORD

THESE GIFTS HAVE A DIRECT RELATION WITH THE SCRIPTURES.

1. APOSTLESHIP – THE ABILITY TO BEGIN A NEW WORK FOR THE LORD THROUGH THE MINISTRY OF THE WORD.

2. PROPHECY – THE ABILITY TO PROCLAIM OR PREACH THE WORD OF GOD.

3. EVANGELISM – THE ABILITY TO PRESENT CHRIST IN SUCH A WAY THAT MEN USUALLY RESPOND BY FAITH.

4. PASTOR-TEACHER – THE ABILITY TO CARE FOR A MAN'S SPIRITUAL NEEDS THROUGH TEACHING THE WORD OF GOD. THE ABILITY TO NURTURE OTHERS IN TRUTH.

5. TEACHING – THE ABILITY TO ANALYZE AND INTERPRET GOD'S TRUTH AND COMMUNICATE IT CLEARLY AND SYSTEMATICALLY.

6. EXHORTATION – THE ABILITY TO MOTIVATE PEOPLE TO ACTION, NORMALLY USING THE AUTHORITY OF GOD'S WORD.

7. WISDOM – THE ABILITY TO APPLY GOD'S TRUTH TO LIFE.

8. KNOWLEDGE – THE ABILITY TO KNOW TRUTH BY THE IMPRESSION OF THE HOLY SPIRIT.

9. DISCERNMENT OF SPIRITS – THE ABILITY TO DISCERN THE SPIRITS OF TRUTH AND ERROR.

10. MUSIC – THE ABILITY TO EXPRESS ONE'S RELATIONSHIP TO GOD THROUGH MUSIC.

MINISTRY OF DIRECTING OTHERS

1. LEADERSHIP (ADMINISTRATION) – THE ABILITY TO LEAD OTHERS AND MANAGE THE AFFAIRS OF THE CHURCH.

2. FAITH – THE ABILITY TO TRUST GOD BEYOND THE PROBABLE AND RAISE THE VISION OF OTHERS.

MINISTRY OF HELPING

1. SERVING – THE ABILITY TO GIVE ASSISTANCE OR AID IN ANY WAY THAT BRINGS STRENGTH OR ENCOURAGEMENT TO OTHERS.

2. GIVING – THE ABILITY TO MAKE AND DISTRIBUTE MONEY TO FURTHER THE CAUSE OF GOD.

3. SHOWING MERCY – THE ABILITY TO WORK JOYFULLY WITH THOSE WHOM THE MAJORITY IGNORES.

4. CRAFTSMANSHIP – THE ABILITY TO WORK WITH ONE'S HANDS FOR THE BENEFIT OF OTHERS.

5. HEALINGS – THE ABILITY TO HEAL A PERSON SPIRITUALLY, EMOTIONALLY, OR PHYSICALLY.

MINISTRY OF THE SPECTACULAR

1. MIRACLES – THE ABILITY TO PERFORM ACTS CONTRARY TO NATURAL LAWS, WITH POWER BEYOND HUMAN CAPACITY.

2. TONGUES – THE ABILITY TO SPEAK IN A LANGUAGE UNLEARNED BY THE SPEAKER.

3. INTERPRETATION – THE ABILITY TO INTERPRET THE MEANING OF A TONGUE, THOUGH THE INTERPRETER HASN'T LEARNED THE LANGUAGE.

WHOSE WISDOM?

WISDOM IS SUPREME; THEREFORE GET
WISDOM.
PROVERBS 4: 7

WISDOM PROTECTS US FROM THE DANGERS
OF KNOWLEDGE.

POTENTIAL IS DORMANT ABILITY.

(The word dormant literally means "that which
is, but it is just lying there below its full
strength, unused.")

📖 IT IS ALSO RESERVED POWER, UNTAPPED
STRENGTH AND UNUSED SUCCESS.

📖 POTENTIAL IS EVERYTHING THAT A

THING IS, THAT HAS NOT YET BEEN SEEN

OR MANIFESTED.

📖 EVERYTHING IN LIFE BEGINS AS

POTENTIAL.

📖 ALL THINGS HAVE THE POTENTIAL TO FULFILL THEMSELVES, BECAUSE GOD CREATED EVERYTHING WITH POTENTIAL.

📖 THERE IS NO FULFILLMENT IN LIFE WITHOUT UNDERSTANDING THE REASON FOR BEING

📖 IF WE WANT TO KNOW THE REAL POTENTIAL OF SOMETHING, WE FIRST HAVE TO KNOW WHAT THAT THING WAS CREATED TO DO.

WHAT IS POTENTIAL?

THE ABORTION OF POTENTIAL IS THE DEATH
OF THE FUTURE.

POTENTIAL IS ...

- UNEXPOSED ABILITY
- RESERVED POWER
- UNTAPPED STRENGTH
- CAPPED CAPABILITIES
- UNUSED SUCCESS
- DORMANT GIFTS
- HIDDEN TALENTS
- LATENT POWER
- WHAT YOU CAN DO THAT YOU HAVEN'T YET DONE
- WHERE YOU CAN GO THAT YOU HAVEN'T GONE YET
- WHO YOU CAN BE THAT YOU HAVEN'T YET BEEN

📖 WHAT YOU CAN IMAGINE THAT YOU HAVEN'T YET IMAGINED

📖 HOW FAR YOU CAN REACH THAT YOU HAVEN'T YET REACHED

📖 WHAT YOU CAN SEE THAT YOU HAVEN'T YET SEEN

📖 WHAT YOU CAN ACCOMPLISH THAT YOU HAVEN'T YET ACCOMPLISHED

TEST FOR LEADERSHIP POTENTIAL

RATE YOURSELF ON THE FOLLOWING CHART
AND CHECK YOU LEADERSHIP POTENTIAL.

YES   NO   SOMETIMES

1. INDEPENDENT DECISION MAKING

2. GOVERN YOURSELF

3. ABILITY TO CONTROL ANGER

4. CONQUER YOURSELF

5. CREATIVELY HANDLE DISAPPOINTMENTS

6. INSPIRES CONFIDENCE

7. RELIABLE

8. CORRECTOR

9. MOBILIZING

10. CONCILIATOR

11. ANTAGONIZING

12. DEVELOP RELATIONSHIPS

13. UNCONDITIONAL ACCEPTANCE OF OTHERS

14. SELF-CONFIDENT

15. APPROACHABLE

16. EGO STRENGTH

17. CENTERED

18. FORGIVING
19. PURPOSEFUL
20. ENCOURAGING
21. RESPONSIBLE

WHAT HAPPENED TO THE REAL YOU?

WHEN A MAN PUTS A LIMIT ON WHAT HE CAN

BE,

HE HAS PUT A LIMIT ON WHAT HE WILL BE.

IN THE BEGINNING, GOD CREATED MAN BY

SPEAKING TO HIMSELF.

HE TOOK A LITTLE BIT OF HIMSELF AND PUT

IT INTO

THE FIRST MAN SO ADAM WOULD BE LIKE

HIM

AND COULD SHARE IN HIS LIFE.

PRINCIPLES

1. EVERYTHING THAT WAS AND IS, WAS IN GOD.

2. GOD IS THE SOURCE OF ALL POTENTIAL.

3. ALL THINGS WERE FORMED AT GOD'S COMMAND SO THE INVISIBLE BECAME VISIBLE.

4. GOD PLANNED THE WORLD IN HIS MIND BEFORE SPEAKING IT INTO EXISTENCE.

PRINCIPLES

1. SATAN DESTROYED MAN'S POTENTIAL TO BE LIKE HIS CREATOR.

2. SATAN DISTORTED MAN'S SELF-CONCEPT – HIS ESTEEM FOR THE BEAUTIFUL CREATION GOD MADE HIM TO BE.

3. SATAN DESTROYED MAN'S TRUE INTELLIGENCE, WHICH IS A SPIRITUAL RELATIONSHIP WITH GOD.

4. WHEN SATAN CRIPPLED MAN'S REAL INTELLIGENCE, MAN LOOKED OUTSIDE HIMSELF TO FIND KNOWLEDGE.

5. SIN CLOGS OUR POTENTIAL

6. JESUS CAME TO BRING US ABUNDANT, REFRESHING, NEW LIFE.

PRINCIPLES

1. GOD CREATED EVERYTHING WITH POTENTIAL.

2. NOTHING IN LIFE IS INSTANT.

3. EVERYTHING IN LIFE HAS THE POTENTIAL TO FULFILL ITS PURPOSE.

4. DON'T BE SATISFIED WITH WHAT YOU NOW ARE.

5. DON'T DIE WITHOUT USING YOUR FULL POTENTIAL.

6. THE GREATEST THREAT TO PROGRESS IS YOUR LAST SUCCESSFUL ACCOMPLISHMENT.

SESSION 3

THE ATTITUDE OF LEADERSHIP

DISCUSSION QUESTIONS

1. WHAT ARE SOME OF THE BEHAVIORAL PATTERNS THAT PEOPLE LIKE FOR A LEADER TO POSSESS?

2. WHAT ARE SOME OF THE BEHAVIORAL PATTERNS THAT PEOPLE DISLIKE IN A LEADER?

PEOPLE LIKE FOR A LEADER TO BE

FRIENDLY

TRUTHFUL

HARD-WORKING

OPEN, YET TACTFUL

CARING

SUPPORTIVE

COMMITTED

ENTHUSIASTIC

TRUSTING

GROUP-ORIENTED

EMOTIONALLY MATURE

SELF-CONFIDENT

201

PEOPLE DISLIKE A LEADER FOR BEING

UNFRIENDLY

AUTHORITARIAN

MANIPULATIVE

LAZY

TACTLESS

UNFEELING

LAISSEZ-FAIRE

EMOTIONLESS

SUSPICIOUS

UNSURE

EMOTIONALLY IMMATURE

BASIC ENDEAVORS OF A LEADER

📖 INVOLVE IN DECISION-MAKING THOSE WHO WILL BE AFFECTED.

📖 BE FLEXIBLE IN MEETING CHANGING GROUP NEEDS.

📖 DISTRIBUTE LEADERSHIP RESPONSIBILITIES WIDELY AMONG RESPONSIBLE PEOPLE RATHER THAN CENTRALIZING RESPONSIBILITIES AMONG A FEW.

📖 SUPPORT GROUP VALUES WHEN APPROPRIATE AND CHALLENGE THEM WHEN NECESSARY.

📖 LEARN FROM AND NOT BE INHIBITED BY THE POSSIBILITY OF FAILURE.

📖 MAKE DECISIONS BASED ON INFORMATION AND EVIDENCE RATHER THAN ON EMOTION.

📖 MAINTAIN A BALANCED CONCERN FOR THE INDIVIDUAL AND FOR THE GROUP.

📖 ENCOURAGE THE DEVELOPMENT AND USE OF INDIVIDUAL GIFTS.

- 📖 LEAD PERSONS TO ESTABLISH AND ASSIST THEM IN ACHIEVING COMMON GOALS.

- 📖 MAINTAIN A HEALTHY RELATIONSHIP BETWEEN TASK AND MAINTENANCE ACTIVITIES IN HIS OWN LIFE AS WELL AS IN ORGANIZATIONAL LIFE.

Seven Principles of Servant-Leadership

Principle#1 Servant leaders humble themselves and wait for God to exalt them

Principle#2 Servant leaders follow Jesus rather than seek a position

Principle#3 Servant leaders give up personal rights to find greatness in service to others

Principle#4 Servant leaders can risk serving others because they trust that God is in control of their lives

Principle#5 Servant leaders take up Jesus' towel of servanthood to meet the needs of others

Principle#6 Servant leaders share responsibility and authority with others to meet a greater need

Principle#7 Servant leaders multiply their leadership by empowering others to lead

SESSION 4

THE NEEDS AND PROCESS OF LEADERSHIP

CHARACTERISTICS OF A HEALTHY RELATIONSHIP

1. MUTUALITY

A relationship cannot exist within one
person; there must be exchanges
between two persons.

2. INITIATIVE

Seek to make the first move

3. RESPECT

Being considerate of the other person's
personal space is important.
Therefore, we need to ask
permission, wait to be invited, and
otherwise be respectful of the rights
of other people

BENEFITS OF RELATIONS

1.   STIMULATION

Relationship provide stimulation to our senses and to our sense of well-being

2.   AFFIRMATION

The most confident person needs affirmation from others. Emotional support is provided when affirmation is given. We develop a sense of self when we see approval reflected in the eyes of someone who affirms us.

3.   RECOGNITION

Positive relationships gives us a sense of well-being. Theologically speaking, this is what God does for us in Christ.

4.   CONSULTATION

Relationship are a source for information, feedback, and clarification.

5.   CONSOLATION

Emotional support in time of crisis is available through relationship

6.   REALIZATION

Relationship provides a place to share that realization which gives it meaning

7.   CONVERSATION

Listening and talking, understanding and being understood is life enhancing-different points of view; different outlooks, different experiences enrich one's life.

8.   COMMUNION

Communion means–joined together. When joined together in relationship information, feelings and opinions are communicated in a never-ending flow.

CARY GEORGE OF THE CHARLES E FULLER INSTITUTE IDENTIFIES 4 PRIMARY FUNCTIONS THAT TAKE PLACE IN GROUPS.

1. Loving;

2. Learning;

3. Doing;

4. Deciding

📖 Loving indicates sharing, encouraging, and relating positively to one another

📖 Learning includes teaching as well as studying and seeking information

📖 Doing means putting feet on faith in a variety of ways, including missions projects and involvement

📖 Deciding/maintaining are the methods of conducting its business affairs, arranging and agenda, securing a commitment to common action, and accomplishing action items.

THERE ARE THREE REASONS WHY JESUS COMMANDED CONTROL OF HIS TIME.

1. He understood His mission

2. Jesus realized that time must be set aside for gathering power and inner strength

3. He budgeted his time, giving priority to the most important things.

PROPER WAYS TO OVERCOME
POOR TIME MANAGEMENT:

1. Put first things first

2. Proper planning (give time to God)

3. Control your time

4. Don't over burden yourself

5. Don't fall prey to procrastination

RUNNING THE MEETING

📖 MEETINGS ARE CALLED FOR

PURPOSE

📖 THERE MUST BE A TIME AND

PLACE

📖 DISPLAY MEETING TIME PLAN

📖 ADHERE TO THE SCHEDULE

📖 WORK THE AGENDA

📖 CLOSE ON TIME

HOW TO MAKE ORGANIZATION WORK

📖 KEEP IT SIMPLE

📖 PUT DUTIES IN WRITING

📖 ELIMINATE OVERLAPPING DUTIES

📖 MAKE SURE EACH ORGANIZATION
   HAS A MEANINGFUL JOB TO DO

📖 DON'T BYPASS PEOPLE IN THE
   ORGANIZATION

📖 PUT BEST WORKERS AT KEY
   POSITIONS

☐ HELP PEOPLE SEE THE BIG PICTURE

☐ SET UP OPPORTUNITY FOR
COMMUNICATION

☐ CONTINUALLY EVALUATE YOUR
ORGANIZATION

☐ ASK FOR REPORTS

MAKING ASSIGNMENTS

EIGHT POINTS TO REMEMBER WHEN

MAKING ASSIGNMENTS

1. Be specific, give clear directions, and do not assume that the volunteer has any knowledge of the job.

2. Tell what the job involves in time and energy.

3. Tell each volunteer the kinds of task that must be done, and, if applicable, mention the need for public appearances.

4. When making an assignment, make certain to have available any materials the volunteer will need in order to do the job.

5. Set a time to begin and a time to end each job.

6. When volunteers are working, have someone available for assistance by phone or in person – incase unforeseen problems occur.

7. The person who makes assignments should evaluate the quality of work done by every volunteer on every job.

8. The person who makes assignments should note any problems encountered by volunteers on any job.

JOB DESCRIPTIONS

PASTOR

Principle Function. – The pastor is responsible to the church to proclaim the gospel of Jesus Christ, to teach the biblical revelation, to engage in pastoral care ministries, to provide administrative leadership in all areas of church life, and to act as the chief administrator of the paid staff.

RESPONSIBILITIES

1. Plan and conduct the worship services; prepare and deliver sermons; lead in observance of ordinances.

2. Lead the church in an effective program of witnessing and in a caring ministry for persons in the church and community.

3. Visit members and prospects.

4. Conduct counseling sessions; perform wedding ceremonies; conduct funerals.

5. Service as chairman of the Church Council to

lead in planning, organizing, directing, coordinating, and evaluating the total program of the church.

6. Work with deacons, church officers, and committees as they perform their assigned responsibilities; train and lead the deacons in a program of family ministries.

7. Act as moderator of church business meetings.

8. Cooperate with associational, state, and denominational leaders in matters of mutual interest and concern; keep the church informed of denominational development; represent the church in civic matters.

9. Serve as chief administrator of the paid church staff; supervise the work of assigned paid staff workers.

MINISTER OF EDUCATION

Principle Function. – The minister of education is responsible to the pastor for providing staff leadership to the entire church educational program. This involves assisting church program leaders in planning, conducting, and evaluating a comprehensive ministry of Christian education in support of the mission and objectives of the church.

RESPONSIBILITIES

1. Lead the church in planning, conducting, and evaluating a comprehensive program of Christian education.
2. Serve as education resource person and advisor to the leaders of church program and service organizations such as Sunday School, Church Training, Woman's Missionary Union, Brotherhood, church library, and church recreation.

3. Serve as educational resource person and advisor to the committees of the church as requested.
4. Work with the church Nominating Committee to select, enlist, and train qualified leaders.
5. Coordinate the production of informational and public relations materials such as church publications and news releases.
6. Develop special educational and training projects such as camps, retreats, and study seminars for various age groups within the congregation.
7. Lead the church to be aware of the educational and curriculum materials available and lead the church to choose the most suitable.
8. Assist the pastor in planning, conducting, and evaluating congregational services as requested.
9. Serve on the Church Council.
10. Supervise appropriate church staff members, such as age-group directors, recreation leaders, educational secretary, and custodian

11. Keep informed on methods, materials, principles, procedures, promotion and administration as related to the education program.

MINISTER OF MUSIC

Principle Function. –The minister of music is responsible to the pastor for the development and promotion of the music program of the church.

RESPONSIBILITIES

1. Direct the planning, organizing, conducting, and evaluating of a comprehensive music program including choirs, vocal and/or instrumental ensembles.
2. Supervise the work of assigned paid staff workers.
3. Cooperate with the church Nominating Committee to enlist and train leaders for the church music ministry including graded choir workers, song leaders, and accompanists for the church education organizations.
4. Lead in planning and promoting a graded choir program; direct and coordinate the work of lay choir directors; direct adult, youth, and other choirs as needed.
5. Serve as a member of the Church Council; coordinate the music program with the organizational calendar and emphases of the church.
6. Assist the pastor in planning all services of worship.

7. Give direction to a music ministry plan of visitation.

8. Arrange and provide music for weddings, funerals, special projects, ministries, and other church-related activities upon request.

9. Plan, organize, and promote choir tours, mission trips, camps, festivals, workshops, clinics, and programs for the various choirs.

10. Maintain music library, materials, supplies, musical instruments, and other equipment.

11. Keep informed on music methods, materials, promotion, and administration.

12. Prepare an annual music budget for approval; administer the approved budget.

13. Cooperate with associational and state leaders in promoting activities of mutual interest.

MINISTER OF YOUTH DIRECTOR OF YOUTH EDUCATION

Principal Function. – The director of youth work is responsible to the minister of education for assisting church program organizations to develop a comprehensive program of youth education. He or she consults with other staff members concerning activities, policies and procedures that relate to their areas of responsibility.

RESPONSIBILITIES

1. Counsel with church program organization leaders in planning, conducting, and evaluating a youth education ministry and in enlisting appropriate youth workers.

2. Conduct special training projects for youth workers in proper relationship to the Church Training program.

3. Advise in the use of program materials,

equipment, supplies and space by youth groups in all church program organizations.

4. Work with the director of library services and the director of the recreation service to provide needed services.

5. Assist with planning and conducting special projects (such as camps and retreats) for youth program organization groups.

6. Work with organization leaders to coordinate visitation for the Youth Division and lead workers to visit prospects and absentees.

7. Work with program leaders and teachers and appropriate staff members to resolve philosophical, procedural, and scheduling problems in the Youth Division.

Note: This description could be used for any age-group specialist; simply substitute the appropriate age group for "youth."

OVERVIEW: THE EIGHT LAWS OF LEADERSHIP

Towns, Elmer. The 8 Laws of Leadership. Lynchburg, VA: Church Growth Institute, 1992.

LAW ONE: THE LAW OF DREAMS

Descriptive Statement:

People follow a leader who directs them to a desirable objective.

Prescriptive Statement:

The leader must direct followers to a desirable objective.

Slogan:

When people buy into your dreams, they buy into your leadership.

LAW TWO: THE LAW OF REWARDS

Descriptive Statement:

People follow a leader who provides them rewards from their self-chosen goal.

Prescriptive Statement:

The leader must reward those who follow him.

Slogan:

The things that get rewarded, get done.

LAW THREE: THE LAW OF CREDIBILITY

Descriptive Statement:

People follow a leader when they have confidence in his plans.

Prescriptive Statement:

The leader must have a credibility plan to reach the objective.

Slogan:

The leader who believes in his followers has people who believe in him.

LAW FOUR: THE LAW OF COMMUNICATION

Descriptive Statement:

People follow a leader who effectively communicates his plan to reach the objective.

Prescriptive Statement:

The leader must effectively communicate his plan to reach the objective.

Slogan:

People follow a leader who give clear directions to his followers.

LAW FIVE: THE LAW OF ACCOUNTABILITY

Descriptive Statement:

People follow a leader who gives them responsibility to help reach the objective.

Prescriptive Statement:

The leader must know the contribution that his followers make to help reach the goal.

Slogan:

People don't do what you expect, but what you inspect.

LAW SIX: THE LAW OF MOTIVATION

Descriptive Statement:

People follow a leader who gives them compelling reasons to reach the objective.

Prescriptive Statement:

The leader must motivate followers to accomplish the objective.

Slogan:

People follow when you have given them a reason to work.

LAW SEVEN: THE LAW OF PROBLEM-SOLVING

Descriptive Statement:

People follow a leader who gives solutions to problems that hinder them from reaching the objective.

Prescriptive Statement:

The leader must solve problems that hinder followers from reaching their objective.

Slogan:

The more barriers that frustrate your followers, the less likely they are to reach the goal.

LAW EIGHT: THE LAW OF DECISION-MAKING

Descriptive Statement:

People follow a leader who gives answers to the decisions involving their objective.

Prescriptive Statement:

The leader must make good decisions that move followers toward the objective.

Slogan:

Leaders make good decisions on good information, bad decisions on bad information, and lucky decisions on no information.

Eastern Star Program against Guns and Gang Violence

SESSION 5

THE COST AND REWARD OF LEADERSHIP

MASLOW'S HIERARCHY OF NEEDS

- 📖 SELF ACTUALIZATION NEEDS

- 📖 ESTEEM NEED

- 📖 BELONGING NEEDS

- 📖 SAFETY NEEDS

- 📖 PHYSIOLOGICAL NEEDS

THE PRICE OF LEADERSHIP

1. Personal sacrifice

2. Rejection

3. Criticism

4. Loneliness

5. Pressure and perplexity

6. Mental and physical fatigue

7. Price paid by others

ESSENTIAL QUALITIES FOR LEADERSHIP

1. Discipline

2. Vision

3. Common Sense

4. Decisiveness

5. Fortitude

6. Humility

7. Sense of Humor

8. Indignation

9. Patience and endurance

10. Fellowship

11. Discretion

12. Inspirational Power

ENDNOTES

[i]Kentucky State Data Center, *1990 Census of Population and Housing*: *Profile 1 – Selected Characteristics of the Population,* University of Louisville Archives. Summary Tape File 3; Profile 6, Selected Characteristics by Education Attainment; Area: Zip Codes 40210 and 40211.

[ii]Tex Sample, *U.S. Lifestyles and Mainline Churches* (Louisville: John Knox Press, 1990), 60.

[iii]Ibid., 61

[iv]Ibid., 60.

[v]Ibid., 61.

[vi]*1990 Census of Population and Housing*, Tape File 3; Profile 6.

[vii]The acronym LTM will refer to leadership training model.

[viii]The term Eastern Star will refer to the Eastern Star Baptist Church unless otherwise stated.

[ix]William L. Holliday, ed., *A Concise Hebrew and Aramaic Lexicon of the Old Testament* (Grand Rapids: William B. Eerdmans Publishing Co, 1988), 380.

[x]J. Philip Hyatt, *The New Century Bible Commentary* (Grand Rapids: Eerdmans Publishing, 1971), 194.

[xi]Roy L. Honeycutt, Jr., Exodus in vol. 1 of *The Broadman Bible Commentary, rev. ed.,* ed. Clifton J. Allen (Nashville: Broadman Press, 1969), 388.

[xii]XXXXXX, Exodus in vol. 1 of *The New Interpreter's Bible*, ed. George A. Buttrick (New

York: Abingdon Press, 1994), 827.

[xiii]Ibid., 828.

[xiv]Ibid.

[xv]Ibid.

[xvi]Honeycutt, *Exodus*, 388.

[xvii]Holladay, *A Concise Hebrew and Aramaic Lexicon*, 74.

[xviii]Ibid.

[xix]Ibid.

[xx]Ibid.

[xxi]J. I. Packer and M.C. Tenny, eds., *Illustrated Manners and Customs of the Bible* (Nashville: Thomas Nelson Publishers, 1997), 319.

[xxii]Ibid., 320.

[xxiii]Buttrick, *New Interpreter's Bible Commentary*; Volume 1, Exodus, 827.

[xxiv]Packer and Tenny, *Illustrated Manners and Customs*, 381.

[xxv]Ibid., 382.

[xxvi]Ibid., 380.

[xxvii]Buttrick, *Exodus*, 827.

[xxviii] Ibid.

[xxix]C. Gene Wilkes, *Jesus on Leadership: Becoming a Servant Leader* (Nashville: Lifeway Press, 1996), 24.

[xxx]Ibid., 24.

[xxxi]Ibid., 25.

[xxxii]G. R. Beasley-Murray, *2 Corinthians* in vol. 11 of *The Broadman Bible Commentary*, ed. Clifton J. Allen (Nashville: Broadman Press, 1971) 153.

xxxiiiF. F. Bruce and E. K. Simpson, *Commentary on the Epistle to the Ephesians and the Colossians* (Grand Rapids: Eerdmans, 1979), 84.

xxxivIbid., 85.

xxxvIbid., 86.

xxxviBeasley-Murray, *1 Corinthians*, 155.

xxxviiIbid.

xxxviiiIbid.

xxxixIbid.

xlIbid.

xliIbid.,156.

xliiIbid.

xliiiIbid.

xlivIbid., 157.

xlvRick Yohn, *Discover your Spiritual Gift and Use It* (Wheaton: Tyndale House, 1974), 143.

xlviIbid.

xlviiIbid.

xlviiiIbid., 144.

xlixIbid.

lIbid., 145.

liIbid.

liiIbid., 146.

liiiIbid.

livIbid., 148.

lvIbid.

lviIbid., 149.

lviiIbid., 150.

lviiiIbid., 151.

lixIbid., 152.

lxIbid.

lxiIbid.

lxiiIbid.

lxiiiIbid.

lxivIbid.

lxvIbid.

lxviIbid., 152-53.

lxviiAndrew T. Lincoln, *Ephesians* in vol. 42 of *Word Biblical Commentary*, ed. David A Hubbard and Glen W. Barker (Dallas: Word Books Publisher, 1990), 267.

lxviiiIbid.

lxixIbid.

lxxJohn Phillips, *Exploring Ephesians* (Neptune, NJ: Loizeaux Brothers, 1993), 119.

lxxiIbid.

lxxiiPheme Perkins, *Ephesians* in vol. XI of *Abingdon New Testament Commentaries, ed., D. Moody Smith* (Nashville, Abingdon Press; 1997), 100.

lxxiiiC. Gene Wilkes, *Jesus on Leadership: Becoming a Servant Leader* (Nashville: Lifeway Press, 1997), 36.

lxxivIbid., 9-10.

lxxvWilliam Beausay II, *The Leadership Genius of Jesus* (Nashville: Nelson Publishers, 1997), 23.

lxxviBob Riner and Ray Pritchard, *More Leadership Lessons of Jesus* (Nashville: Broadman and Holman Publishers, 1998), 127.

lxxviiWilkes, *Jesus on Leadership*, 9.

lxxviiiIbid., 11-12.

lxxixIbid., 231.

lxxxIbid., 232.

lxxxiLovett H. Weems Jr., *Church Leadership: Vision, Team, Culture, and Integrity* (Nashville: Abingdon Press, 1993), 16.

lxxxiiPaul Powell, *Getting the Lead out of Leadership* (Tyler TX: The Southern Baptist Annuity Board, 1997), 7.

lxxxiiiR. Paul Stevens and Phil Collins, *The Equipping Pastor* (New York: Alban Institute, 1993), 8.

lxxxivMyles Monroe, *Becoming a Leader: Everyone Can Do It* (Bakersfield, CA: Pneuma Publishing, 1993), 36.

lxxxvIbid.

lxxxviLovett H. Weems Jr., *Church Leadership: Vision, Team, Culture, and Integrity* (Nashville: Abingdon Press, 1993), 26.

lxxxviiWalt Kallestad, *The Everyday Anytime Guide to Christian Leadership* (Minneapolis: Augsburg, 1994), 12.

lxxxviiiIbid.

lxxxixC. Gene Wilkes, *Jesus on Leadership: Becoming A Servant Leader* (Nashville: Lifeway Press, 1996), 4.

xcIbid.

xciIbid., 95.

xciiTed W. Engstrom, *The Making of a Christian Leader* (Grand Rapids: Zondervan Publishing Co., 1976), 23.

[xciii]Ibid.

[xciv]Ibid.,26.

[xcv]Ibid.

[xcvi]Leith Anderson, *Dying for Change* (Minneapolis: Bethany House Publishers, 1998.), 190.

[xcvii]Sermon-Romans 12:1 preached by Rev. Alex J. Moses, Sr., at Highland Park Missionary Baptist Church, Louisville, Kentucky; Revival 1999; Subject: "Where there is no intimacy with God, There is no Commitment"

[xcviii]Reginald M. McDonough, *Working with Volunteer Leaders in the Church* (Nashville: Broadman Press, 1976), 12.

[xcix]Ibid., 13

[c]Ibid.

[ci]Ibid.

[cii]Ibid., 15.

[ciii]Ibid.

[civ]Ibid., 16.

[cv]Ibid.

[cvi]Ibid., 17.

[cvii]Ibid.

[cviii]Ibid., 18.

[cix]Ibid.

[cx]Ibid., 20.

[cxi]Ibid., 20.

[cxii]Ibid., 20-23.

[cxiii]Ibid., 23.

[cxiv]Ibid.

cxvIbid., 24.

cxviIbid., 28

cxviiIbid., 29.

cxviiiIbid.

cxixJan Chartier, *Developing Leadership in the Teaching Church* (Valley Forge, PA: Judson Press, 1985), 54.

cxxIbid.

cxxiIbid., 55.

cxxiiIbid., 56.

cxxiiiIbid., 57.

cxxivIbid.

cxxvIbid.

cxxviIbid.

cxxviiIbid.

cxxviiiIbid.

cxxixIbid., 58.

cxxxIbid.

cxxxiIbid.

cxxxiiIbid., 59.

cxxxiiiIbid, 59.

cxxxivStated by Dr. Lincoln Bingham at a Central District Baptist Association Banquet held at the Galt House April 14, 1990 honoring local pastors for 25 year of service. He then encouraged all pastors to consider the soil (location and demographics) of the church and community where one pastors.

cxxxvStatement first made during a church business meeting, January 1989.

[cxxxvi]See Appendix 1 for complete Needs Assessment Survey as issued.

[cxxxvii]See Appendix 2.

[cxxxviii]"Blacks Continue to Fall Behind White Students," *Lexington Herald*, June 25, 2001, 1.

[cxxxix]Carolyn N. Connor, interview by Alex James Moses, Louisville, KY, 15 July 2001.

[cxl]Doris Cox, interview by Alex James Moses, Louisville, KY, 15 July 2001.

[cxli] See Appendix 1 for complete Evaluation Questionnaire as issued.

BIBLIOGRAPHY

Anderson, Leith. *Dying for Change*. Minneapolis: Bethany House Publishers, 1998.

Baker, Benjamin S. *Feeding the Sheep*. Nashville: Broadman Press, 1985.

_____. *Shepherding the Sheep*. Nashville: Broadman Press, 1983.

Beasley-Murray. G. R. *2 Corinthians* In vol. 11 of *The Broadman Commentary*, Edited by Clifton J. Allen, 1-76. Nashville: Broadman Press, 1971.

Beausay, William II. *The Leadership Genius of Jesus*. Nashville: Thomas Nelson Publishers, 1997.

Belleville, Linda L. *Women Leaders and the Church*. Grand Rapids: Baker Books, 2000.

Bennis, Warren, and Burt Nanus. *Leaders.* New York: Harper & Row, 1997.

Bickers, Dennis, W. *The Tentmaking Pastor*. Grand Rapids: Baker Books, 2000.

Bratcher, Robert, and Eugene A. Nida. *A Handbook of Paul's Letter to the Ephesians*. New York: United Bible Societies, 1982.

XXXXXXX. *Exodus* In vol. 1 *New Interpreter's Bible Commentary*; Edited by George Arthur Buttrick, xxx-xxx. .Nashville: Abington Press, 1994.

Briner, Bob, and Ray Pritchard. *The Leadership Lessons of Jesus: A Timeless Model for Today's Leaders*. Nashville: Broadman and Holman Publishers, 1997.

_____. *More Leadership Lessons of Jesus: A Timeless Model for Today's Leaders.*. Nashville: Broadman and Holman Publishers, 1998.

Bruce, F. F., and E. K. Simpson. *Commentary on the Epistle to the Ephesians and the Colossians.* Grand Rapids: Eerdmans, 1979.

Caldwell, Kirbyjon H. *The Gospel of Good Success.* New York: Simon and Schuster, 1999.

Callahan, Kennon L. *Effective Church Leadership.* San Francisco: Jossey-Bass Publishers, 1990.

Chappel, Bryan. *Christ-Centered Preaching.* Grand Rapids: Baker Books, 1999.

Chartier, Jan. *Developing Leadership in the Teaching Church.* Valley Forge: Judson Press, 1985.

Cone, James H. *The Spirituals and the Blues.* Maryknoll, NY: Orbis Books, 1999.

Conger, Jay A., and R. N. Kanungo. *Charismatic Leadership.* San Francisco: Jossey-Bass, 1988.

Dale, Robert D. *Pastoral Leadership.* Nashville: Abingdon Press, 1986.

Damon, Roberta McBride. *Relationship Skills.* Birmingham: WMU, 1993.

DeHaan, M. R. *Law or Grace.* Grand Rapids: Zondervan Publishing House, 1965.

Dinkmeyer, Don, and Daniel Eckstein. *Leadership by Encouragement.* Delray Beach, FL: St. Lucie, 1996.

Dobbins, Gaines S. *Learning to Lead.* Nashville: Broadman, 1968.

Dudley, Carl S. *Basic Steps Toward Community Ministry.* New York: The Alban Institute, 1997.

Edge, Findley B. *The Doctrine of the Laity.* Nashville: Convention Press, 1988.

Edwards, Jefferson. *Gifted-Discovering Your Hidden Greatness*. Bakersfield, CA: Pneuma Life Publishing, 1994.

Engstrom, Theodore W. *The Making of a Christian Leader*. Grand Rapids: Zondervan, 1976.

Fitts, Leroy. *A History of Black Baptists*. Nashville: Broadman Press, 1985.

Flake, Floyd, and Donna Marie Williams. *The Way of the Bootstrapper*. San Francisco: HarperCollins Publishers, 1999.

Flynn, Leslie B. *19 Gifts of the Spirit*. Wheaton: Scripture Press, 1974.

Fretheim, Terence E. *Exodus*. Louisville: John Knox Press, 1991.

Gangel, Kenneth O. *Competent to Lead*. Chicago: Moody Press, 1977.

Goatley, David Emmanuel. *Were You There?* Maryknoll, NY: Orbis Books, 1996.

Gool, Robyn. *Proper Attitudes toward Leadership*. Tulsa: Christian Publishing Services, 1987.

Greenleaf, Robert K. *Advices to Servants*. Cambridge: Center for Applied Studies, 1975.

Guns, Geoffrey V. Church. *Financial Management*. Franklin, TN: Providence House Publishers, 1997.

Hagin, Kenneth E. *Plans, Purposes & Pursuits*. Tulsa: Faith Library Publications, 1991.

Hamlin, Judy. *Group Building Skills*. Birmingham: New Hope, 1994.

Harrall, Harriet. *Communication Skills*. Birmingham: New Hope, 1994.

Harris, James H. *Pastoral Theology*. Minneapolis: Fortress Press, 1991.

Harris, Philip B. *The Training Program of a Church.* Nashville: Convention Press, 1966.

Hemphill, Ken. *The Antioch Effect.* Nashville: Broadman and Holman Publishers, 1994.

Herrington, Jim, Mike Bonem, and James H. Furr. *Leading Congregational Change.* San Francisco: Jossey-Bass Publishers, 2000.

Hicks, H. Beecher, Jr. *Preaching through a Storm.* Grand Rapids: Zondervan Publishing House, 1987.

Holladay, William L. *A Concise Hebrew and Aramaic Lexicon of the Old Testament: Based on the First, Second, and Third Editions of the Koehler-Baumgartner Lexicon in Veteris Testamenti Libros.* Grand Rapids: William B. Eerdmans Publishing Co., 1988.

Holloway, Joseph E., ed. *Africanisms in American Culture.* Bloomington: Indiana University Press, 1991.

Hyatt, J. Philip. *Exodus. The New Century Bible Commentary.* Grand Rapids: Eerdmans Publishing, 1971.

Johnson, Douglas W. *Empowering Lay Volunteers.* Nashville: Abingdon Press, 1991.

Johnson, Earl D. *Leadership in the New Testament Church.* Bakersfield,CA : Pneuma Life Publishing, 1993.

_____. *The Care & Feeding of Volunteers.* Nashville: Abingdon Press, 1978.

Johnson, Evelyn. *Shared Leadership: Enabling Church Volunteers to say "Yes."* Atlanta: Presbyterian Publishing House, 1982.

Keller, James. *How to be a Leader by Communicating Your Ideas.* New York: Christopher Books, 1963.

Kelley, Page H. *Exodus: Called for Redemptive Mission*. Nashville: Convention Press, 1977.

Kunjufu, Jawanza. *Black Economics*. Chicago: African American Images, 1991.

Leas, Speed B. *Leadership & Conflict*. Nashville: Abingdon Press, 1982.

Lewis, Phillip V. *Transformational Leadership*. Nashville: Broadman and HolmanPublishers, 1996.

Lincoln, Andrew T. *Ephesians* In vol. 42 of *Word Biblical Commentary,* Edited by. David A. Hubbard and Glenn W. Barker, 222-269. Dallas: Word Books, 1990.

Lincoln, C. Eric, and Lawrence H. Mamiya. *The Black Church in the African American Experience*. Durham: Duke University Press, 1995.

Linthicum, Robert C. *Empowering the Poor*. Monrovia: MARC, 1996.

Lloyd, Debbie. *Time Management*. Birmingham: New Hope, 1994.

Malone, Walter Jr. *An Operative Faith for Oppressed People*. Nashville: The National Baptist Publishing Board, 1987.

Mapson, J. Wendell Jr. *The Ministry of Music in the Black Church*. Valley Forge: Judson Press, 1984.

Martin, Ralph P. Interpretation Bible Commentary. *Ephesians, Colossians, and Philemon*. Atlanta: John Knox Press, 1989.

Massey, Floyd Jr., and Samuel Berry McKinney. *Church Administration in the Black Perspective*. Valley Forge: Judson Press, 1976.

Mayes, Eric A. Jr. *Deacon Training in the Black Church*. Oklahoma City: BEAM Ministries, 1991.

McCalep, George O. Jr. *Breaking the Huddle*. Lithonia: Orman Press, 1997.

251

_____. *Faithful Over a Few Things*. Lithonia: Orman Press, 1996.

McCall, Emmanuel L. ed. "Black Churches Developing Strategies for the 1980's." Atlanta: Home Mission Board, 1982.

_____. *Black Church Lifestyles*. Nashville: Broadman Press, 1986.

_____. ed. "Partners in Ministry." Atlanta: Home Mission Board, 1982.

McClure, John S., and Nancy J. Ramsay, *Telling the Truth*. Cleveland: United Church Press, 1998.

McCumber, W. E. *Everybody into the Field!* Kansas City: Beacon Hill Press, 1995.

McDonough, Reginald. *The ABC's of Church Administration–Study Guide*. Nashville: The Sunday School Board of the Southern Baptist Convention, 1973.

_____. *Keys to Effective Motivation*. Nashville: Broadman Press, 1979.

_____. *Working with Volunteer Leaders in the Church*. Nashville: Broadman Press, 1976.

McSwain, Larry L. and William C. Treadwell, Jr. *Conflict Ministry in the Church*. Nashville: Broadman Press, 1981.

Munroe, Myles. *Becoming a Leader*. Bakersfield, CA: Pneuma Life Publishing, 1993.

_____. *Releasing Your Potential*. Shippensburg, PA: Destiny Image Publishers, 1993.

_____. *Understanding Your Potential*. Shippensburg, PA: Destiny Image Publishers, 1992.

Nance, Terry. *God's Armor Bearer*. Tulsa: Harrison House, 1990.

_____. *God's Armor Bearer*. Book 2. Tulsa: Harrison House, 1994.

Niebuhr, H. Richard. *The Responsible Self*. Louisville: Westminster John Knox Press, 1963.

Packer, J. I., and, M. C. Tenney, eds. *Illustrated Manners and Customs of the Bible*. Nashville: Thomas Nelson Publishers, 1980.

Paris, Peter J. *The Spirituality of African Peoples*. Minneapolis: Fortress Press, 1995.

Parsons, George, and Speed B. Leas. *Understanding Your Congregation as a System*. New York: Alban Institute Publication, 1993.

Perkins, John M. *Beyond Charity*. Grand Rapids: Baker Books, 1996.

Pinder, Richard. *Mobilizing Human Resources*. Bakersfield, CA: Pneuma Life Publishing, 1994.

Plumpp, Sterling. *Black Rituals*. Chicago: Third World Press: 1991.

Powell, Charles. *New Member Training*. Nashville: National Baptist Publishing Board, 1983.

Powell, Paul W. *Getting the Lead out of Leadership*. Tyler, TX: Paul W. Powell, 1977.

_____. *Shepherding the Sheep in Smaller Churches*. Dallas: Annuity Board, 1995.

_____. *Taking the Stew out of Stewardship*. Dallas: Annuity Board, 1996.

Powers, Bruce P. *Christian Leadership*. Nashville: Broadman Press, 1979.

_____. *Church Administration Handbook*. Nashville: Broadman Press, 1985.

Raboteau, Albert J. *Slave Religion*. Oxford: Oxford University Press, 1980.

Reed, Bobbie, and John Westfall. *Building Strong People*. Grand Rapids: Baker House, 1997.

Reed, Gregory J. *Economic Empowerment through the Church*. Grand Rapids: Zondervan Publishing House, 1994.

Roberts, J. Deotis. *Black Theology in Dialogue*. Philadelphia: Westminster Press, 1987.

_____. *Liberation and Reconciliation*. Maryknoll, NY: Orbis, 1994.

_____. *The Prophethood of Black Believers*. Louisville: Westminster/John Knox Press, 1994.

Robinson, Darrell W. *Total Church Life*. Nashville: Broadman & Holman Publishers, 1993.

Sample, Tex. *U.S. Lifestyles and Mainline Churches*. Louisville: Westminster/John Knox Press, 1990.

Sawyer, David. *Work of The Church*. Valley Forge: Judson Press, 1993.

Schaller, Lyle E. *Innovations in Ministry*. Nashville: Abingdon Press, 1994.

_____. *The Seven-Day-a-Week Church*. Nashville: Abingdon Press, 1992.

Schooley, Shirley. *Conflict Management*. Birmingham: New Hope, 1994.

Sherman, Amy L. *Restorers of Hope*. Wheaton: Crossway Books, 1997.

Smith, Wallace C. *The Church in the life of the Black Family*. Valley Forge: Judson Press, 1990.

Stassen, Glen H., D. M. Yeager, and John Howard Yoder. *Authentic Transformation*. Nashville: Abingdon Press, 1996.

Stevens, R. Paul, and Phil Collins. *The Equipping Pastor*. New York: Alban Institute, 1993.

Stewart, Carlyle Fielding, III. *African American Church Growth*. Nashville: Abingdon Press, 1994.

Thomas, Latta R. *Biblical Faith and the Black American*. Valley Forge, PA: Judson Press, 1981.

Toler, Stan, and Alan Nelson. *The Five Star Church*. Ventura: Regal Books, 1999.

Townes, Emilie M., ed. *A Troubling in my Soul*. Maryknoll, NY: Orbis Books, 1997.

Towns, Elmer. *The 8 Laws of Leadership*. Lynchburg, VA: Church Growth Institute, 1992.

Turpie, Bill, ed. *Ten Great Preachers.* Grand Rapids: Baker Books, 2000.

Warren, Rick. *The Purpose Driven Church*. Grand Rapids: Zondervan Publishing House, 1995.

Weems, Lovett H., Jr.. *Church Leadership: Vision, Team, Culture, and Integrity*. Nashville: Abingdon Press, 1993.

West, Cornel. *Race Matters*. Boston: Beacon Press, 1993.

Westing, Harold J. *Church Staff Handbook*. Grand Rapids: Kregel Publications, 1997.

White, Ernest O. *Becoming a Christian Leader*. Nashville: Convention Press, 1985.

Wilkes, C. Gene. *Jesus on Leadership*. Wheaton: Tyndale House Publishers, 1988.

Woodson, Robert L., Sr. The *Triumphs of Joseph*. New York: The Free Press, 1998.

Yohn, Rick. *Discover Your Spiritual Gift and Use It*. Wheaton: Tyndale House Publishers, 1974.

VITA
Alex James Moses, Sr.

PERSONAL

Born: September 1, 1944, Newberry, South Carolina

Parents: Ira M. and Carrie L. Moses

Married: Gertrude M. Murphy, July 3, 1965

Children: Alex James Jr., born December 15, 1965

Marcus Sherrod, born November 18, 1968

Carla Lynn, December born 20, 1969

EDUCATIONAL

Diploma, Richmond, Virginia, 1964.

B.A., Simmons Bible College, Louisville, Kentucky, 1983.

M.A., The Southern Baptist Theological Seminary, 1988.

M.Div. Equivalent, The Southern Baptist Theological Seminary, 1998.

MINISTERIAL

Pastor, Eastern Star Baptist Church,
Louisville, Kentucky, 1984

ORGANIZATIONAL

Simmons Bible College, Faculty Member

Central District Baptist Association, Vice Moderator

Louisville Urban League, Board of Directors

CLOUT, Former Co-President

West Louisville Ministries, Board Member

Interdenominational Ministerial Coalition, Member

Citizens Police Academy, Graduate

Volunteer Instructor, LPD (Officer Training

Division)

Proof

41779513R00153

Made in the USA
Charleston, SC
07 May 2015